# THE QUIRT

B. M. BOWER

# The Quirt

B. M. Bower

© 1st World Library, 2006
PO Box 2211
Fairfield, IA 52556
www.1stworldlibrary.com
First Edition

LCCN: 2006935174

Softcover ISBN: 1-4218-2466-3
Hardcover ISBN: 1-4218-2366-7
eBook ISBN: 1-4218-2566-X

Purchase *"The Quirt"*
as a traditional bound book at:
www.1stWorldLibrary.com/purchase.asp?ISBN=1-4218-2466-3

1st World Library is a literary, educational organization dedicated to:

- Creating a free internet library of downloadable ebooks

- Hosting writing competitions and offering book publishing scholarships.

Interested in more 1st World Library books? contact:
literacy@1stworldlibrary.com
Check us out at: www.1stworldlibrary.com

# 1ˢᵗ World Library Literary Society

## Giving Back to the World

"If you want to work on the core problem, it's early school literacy."

- **James Barksdale, former CEO of Netscape**

"No skill is more crucial to the future of a child, or to a democratic and prosperous society, than literacy."

- **Los Angeles Times**

Literacy... means far more than learning how to read and write... The aim is to transmit... knowledge and promote social participation."

- **UNESCO**

"Literacy is not a luxury, it is a right and a responsibility. If our world is to meet the challenges of the twenty-first century we must harness the energy and creativity of all our citizens."

- **President Bill Clinton**

"Parents should be encouraged to read to their children, and teachers should be equipped with all available techniques for teaching literacy, so the varying needs and capacities of individual kids can be taken into account."

- **Hugh Mackay**

# CONTENTS

I. LITTLE FISH ...................................................................7
II. THE ENCHANTMENT OF LONG DISTANCE.............13
III. REALITY IS WEIGHED AND FOUND WANTING.......19
IV. "SHE'S A GOOD GIRL WHEN SHE AIN'T CRAZY" ....28
V. A DEATH "BY ACCIDENT" .............................................38
VI. LONE ADVISES SILENCE....... .....................................47
VII. THE MAN AT WHISPER .................................................57
VIII. "IT TAKES NERVE JUST TO HANG ON" ...................66
IX. THE EVIL EYE OF THE SAWTOOTH .........................76
X. ANOTHER SAWTOOTH "ACCIDENT" ........................83
XI. SWAN TALKS WITH HIS THOUGHTS .......................93
XII. THE QUIRT PARRIES THE FIRST BLOW.................101
XIII. LONE TAKES HIS STAND .........................................107
XIV. "FRANK'S DEAD"..........................................................114
XV. SWAN TRAILS A COYOTE .........................................123
XVI. THE SAWTOOTH SHOWS ITS HAND....................128
XVII. YACK DON'T LIE..........................................................138
XVIII. "I THINK AL WOODRUFF'S GOT HER" ..............149
XIX. SWAN CALLS FOR HELP .........................................156
XX. KIDNAPPED ..................................................................162
XXI. "OH, I COULD KILL YOU!" ........................................168
XXII. "YACK, I LICK YOU GOOD IF YOU BARK" ...........176
XXIII. "I COULDA LOVED THIS LITTLE GIRL" .............180
XXIV. ANOTHER STORY BEGINS .....................................187

# CHAPTER ONE

## LITTLE FISH

Quirt Creek flowed sluggishly between willows which sagged none too gracefully across its deeper pools, or languished beside the rocky stretches that were bone dry from July to October, with a narrow channel in the center where what water there was hurried along to the pools below. For a mile or more, where the land lay fairly level in a platter-like valley set in the lower hills, the mud that rimmed the pools was scored deep with the tracks of the "TJ up-and-down" cattle, as the double monogram of Hunter and Johnson was called.

A hard brand to work, a cattleman would tell you. Yet the TJ up-and-down herd never seemed to increase beyond a niggardly three hundred or so, though the Quirt ranch was older than its lordly neighbors, the Sawtooth Cattle Company, who numbered their cattle by tens of thousands and whose riders must have strings of fifteen horses apiece to keep them going; older too than many a modest ranch that had flourished awhile and had finished as line-camps of the Sawtooth when the Sawtooth bought ranch and brand for a lump sum that looked big to the rancher, who immediately departed to make himself a new home elsewhere: older than others which had somehow gone to pieces when the rancher died or went to the penitentiary under the stigma of a long sentence as a cattle thief. There were many such, for the Sawtooth, powerful and stern against outlawry, tolerated no pilfering from their thousands.

The less you have, the more careful you are of your possessions. Hunter and Johnson owned exactly a section and a half of land, and for a mile and a half Quirt Creek was fenced upon either side. They hired two men, cut what hay they could from a field which they irrigated, fed their cattle through the cold weather, watched them zealously through the summer, and managed to ship enough beef each fall to pay their grocery bill and their men's wages and have a balance sufficient to buy what clothes they needed, and perhaps pay a doctor if one of them fell ill. Which frequently happened, since Brit was becoming a prey to rheumatism that sometimes kept him in bed, and Frank occasionally indulged himself in a gallon or so of bad whisky and suffered afterwards from a badly deranged digestion.

Their house was a two-room log cabin, built when logs were easier to get than lumber. That the cabin contained two rooms was the result of circumstances rather than design. Brit had hauled from the mountain-side logs long and logs short, and it had seemed a shame to cut the long ones any shorter. Later, when the outside world had crept a little closer to their wilderness - as, go where you will, the outside world has a way of doing - he had built a lean-to shed against the cabin from what lumber there was left after building a cowshed against the log barn.

In the early days, Brit had had a wife and two children, but the wife could not endure the loneliness of the ranch nor the inconvenience of living in a two-room log cabin. She was continually worrying over rattlesnakes and diphtheria and pneumonia, and begging Brit to sell out and live in town. She had married him because he was a cowboy, and because he was a nimble dancer and rode gallantly with silver-shanked spurs ajingle on his heels and a snakeskin band around his hat, and because a ranch away out on Quirt Creek had sounded exactly like a story in a book.

Adventure, picturesqueness, even romance, are recognized and appreciated only at a distance. Mrs. Hunter lost the perspective of romance and adventure, and shed tears because there was sufficient mineral in the water to yellow her week's washing, and for various other causes which she had never foreseen and to which she refused to resign herself.

Came a time when she delivered a shrill-voiced, tear-blurred ultimatum to Brit. Either he must sell out and move to town, or she would take the children and leave him. Of towns Brit knew nothing except the post-office, saloon, cheap restaurant side, - and a barber shop where a fellow could get a shave and hair-cut before he went to see his girl. Brit could not imagine himself actually *living*, day after day, in a town. Three or four days had always been his limit. It was in a restaurant that he had first met his wife. He had stayed three days when he had meant to finish his business in one, because there was an awfully nice girl waiting on table in the Palace, and because there was going to be a dance on Saturday night, and he wanted his acquaintance with her to develop to the point where he might ask her to go with him, and be reasonably certain of a favorable answer.

Brit would not sell his ranch. In this Frank Johnson, old-time friend and neighbor, who had taken all the land the government would allow one man to hold, and whose lines joined Brit's, profanely upheld him. They had planned to run cattle together, had their brand already recorded, and had scraped together enough money to buy a dozen young cows. Luckily, Brit had "proven up" on his homestead, so that when the irate Mrs. Hunter deserted him she did not jeopardize his right to the land.

Brit was philosophical, thinking that a year or so of town life would be a cure. If he missed the children, he was free from tears and nagging complaints, so that his content balanced his loneliness. Frank proved up and came down to live with him, and the partnership began to wear into permanency. Share and share alike, they lived and worked and wrangled together like brothers.

For months Brit's wife was too angry and spiteful to write. Then she wrote acrimoniously, reminding Brit of his duty to his children. Royal was old enough for school and needed clothes. She was slaving for them as she had never thought to slave when Brit promised to honor and protect her, but the fact remained that he was their father even if he did not act like one. She needed at least ten dollars.

Brit showed the letter to Frank, and the two talked it over solemnly while they sat on inverted feed buckets beside the stable, facing the unearthly beauty of a cloud-piled Idaho sunset. They did not feel that they could afford to sell a cow, and two-year-old steers were out of the question. They decided to sell an unbroken colt that a cow-puncher fancied. In a week Brit wrote a brief, matter-of-fact letter to Minnie and enclosed a much-worn ten-dollar banknote. With the two dollars and a half which remained of his share of the sale, Brit sent to a mail-order house for a mackinaw coat, and felt cheated afterwards because the coat was not "wind and water proof" as advertised in the catalogue.

More months passed, and Brit received, by registered mail, a notice that he was being sued for divorce on the ground of non-support. He felt hurt, because, as he pointed out to Frank, he was perfectly willing to support Minnie and the kids if they came back where he could have a chance. He wrote this painstakingly to the lawyer and received no reply. Later he learned from Minnie that she had freed herself from him, and that she was keeping boarders and asking no odds of him.

To come at once to the end of Brit's matrimonial affairs, he heard from the children once in a year, perhaps, after they were old enough to write. He did not send them money, because he seemed never to have any money to send, and because they did not ask for any. Dumbly he sensed, as their handwriting and their spelling improved, that his children were growing up. But when he thought of them they seemed remote, prattling youngsters whom Minnie was forever worrying over and who seemed to have been always under the heels of his horse, or under the wheels of his wagon, or playing with the pitchfork, or wandering off into the sage while he and their distracted mother searched for them. For a long while - how many years Brit could not remember - they had been living in Los Angeles. Prospering, too, Brit understood. The girl, Lorraine - Minnie had wanted fancy names for the kids, and Brit apologized whenever he spoke of them, which was seldom - Lorraine had written that "Mamma has an apartment house." That had sounded prosperous, even at the beginning. And as the years passed and their address remained the same, Brit became fixed in the belief that the Casa Grande was all that its name implied, and perhaps more. Minnie must be getting rich. She had a picture of the place on the stationery which Lorraine used when she wrote him. There were two palm trees in front, with bay windows behind them, and pillars. Brit used to study these magnificences and thank God that Minnie was doing so well. He never could have given her a home like that. Brit sometimes added that he had never been cut out for a married man, anyway.

Old-timers forgot that Brit had ever been married, and late comers never heard of it. To all intents the owners of the Quirt outfit were old bachelors who kept pretty much to themselves, went to town only when they needed supplies, rode old, narrow-fork saddles and grinned scornfully at "swell-forks" and "buckin'-rolls," and listened to all the range gossip without adding so much as an opinion. They never talked politics nor told which candidates received their two votes. They kept the same two men season after season, - leathery old range hands with eyes that saw whatever came within their field of vision, and with the gift of silence, which is rare.

If you know anything at all about cattlemen, you will know that the Quirt was a poor man's ranch, when I tell you that Hunter and Johnson milked three cows and made butter, fed a few pigs on the skim milk and the alfalfa stalks which the saddle horses and the cows disdained to eat, kept a flock of chickens, and sold what butter, eggs and pork they did not need for themselves. Cattlemen seldom do that. More often they buy milk in small tin cans, butter in "squares," and do without eggs.

Four of a kind were the men of the TJ up-and-down, and even Bill Warfield - president and general manager of the Sawtooth Cattle Company, and of the Federal Reclamation Company and several other companies, State senator and general benefactor of the Sawtooth country - even the great Bill Warfield lifted his hat to the owners of the Quirt when he met them, and spoke of them as "the finest specimens of our old, fast-vanishing type of range men." Senator Warfield himself represented the modern type of range man and was proud of his progressiveness. Never a scheme for the country's development was hatched but you would find Senator Warfield closely allied with it, his voice the deciding one when policies and progress were being discussed.

As to the Sawtooth, forty thousand acres comprised their holdings under patents, deeds and long-time leases from the government. Another twenty thousand acres they had access to through the grace of the owners, and there was forest-reserve grazing besides, which the Sawtooth could have if it chose to pay the nominal rental sum. The Quirt ranch was almost surrounded by Sawtooth land of one sort or another, though there was scant grazing in the early spring on the sagebrush wilderness to the south. This needed Quirt Creek for accessible water, and Quirt Creek, save where it ran through cut-bank hills, was fenced within the section and a half of the TJ up-and-down.

So there they were, small fish making shift to live precariously with other small fish in a pool where big fish swam lazily. If one small fish now and then disappeared with mysterious abruptness, the other small fish would perhaps scurry here and there for a time, but few would leave the pool for the safe shallows beyond.

This is a tale of the little fishes.

## CHAPTER TWO

## THE ENCHANTMENT OF LONG DISTANCE

Lorraine Hunter always maintained that she was a Western girl. If she reached the point of furnishing details she would tell you that she had ridden horses from the time that she could walk, and that her father was a cattle-king of Idaho, whose cattle fed upon a thousand hills. When she was twelve she told her playmates exciting tales about rattlesnakes. When she was fifteen she sat breathless in the movies and watched picturesque horsemen careering up and down and around the thousand hills, and believed in her heart that half the Western pictures were taken on or near her father's ranch. She seemed to remember certain landmarks, and would point them out to her companions and whisper a desultory lecture on the cattle industry as illustrated by the picture. She was much inclined to criticism of the costuming and the acting.

At eighteen she knew definitely that she hated the very name Casa Grande. She hated the narrow, half-lighted hallway with its "tree" where no one ever hung a hat, and the seat beneath where no one ever sat down. She hated the row of key-and-mail boxes on the wall, with the bell buttons above each apartment number. She hated the jangling of the hall telephone, the scurrying to answer, the prodding of whichever bell button would summon the tenant asked for by the caller. She hated the meek little Filipino boy who swept that ugly hall every morning. She hated the scrubby palms in front. She hated the pillars where the paint was peeling badly. She hated the conflicting odors that seeped into the atmosphere at certain hours of the day. She hated the three old maids on the third floor and the frowsy woman on the first, who sat on the front steps in her soiled breakfast cap and bungalow apron. She hated the nervous tenant who occupied the apartment just over her mother's three-room-and-bath, and pounded with a broom handle on the floor when Lorraine practised overtime on chromatic scales.

At eighteen Lorraine managed somehow to obtain work in a Western picture, and being unusually pretty she so far distinguished herself that she was given a small part in the next production. Her glorious duty it was to ride madly through the little cow-town "set" to the post-office where the sheriff's posse lounged conspicuously, and there pull her horse to an abrupt stand and point excitedly to the distant hills. Also she danced quite close to the camera in the "Typical Cowboy Dance" which was a feature of this particular production.

Lorraine thereby earned enough money to buy her fall suit and coat and cheap furs, and learned to ride a horse at a gallop and to dance what passed in pictures as a "square dance."

At nineteen years of age Lorraine Hunter, daughter of old Brit Hunter of the TJ up-and-down, became a real "range-bred girl" with a real Stetson hat of her own, a green corduroy riding skirt, gray flannel shirt, brilliant neckerchief, boots and spurs. A third picture gave her further practice in riding a real horse, - albeit an extremely docile animal called Mouse with good reason. She became known on the lot as a real cattle-king's daughter, though she did not know the name of her father's brand and in all her life had seen no herd larger than the thirty head of tame cattle which were chased past the camera again and again to make them look like ten thousand, and which were so thoroughly "camera broke" that they stopped when they were out of the scene, turned and were ready to repeat the performance *ad lib.*

Had she lived her life on the Quirt ranch she would have known a great deal more about horseback riding and cattle and range dances. She would have known a great deal less about the romance of the West, however, and she would probably never have seen a sheriff's posse riding twenty strong and bunched like bird-shot when it leaves the muzzle of the gun. Indeed, I am very sure she would not. Killings such as her father heard of with his lips drawn tight and the cords standing out on the sides of his skinny neck she would have considered the grim tragedies they were, without once thinking of the "picture value" of the crime.

As it was, her West was filled with men who died suddenly in gobs of red paint and girls who rode loose-haired and panting with hand held over the heart, hurrying for doctors, and cowboys and parsons and such. She had seen many a man whip pistol from holster and dare a mob with lips drawn back in a wolfish grin over his white, even teeth, and kidnappings were the inevitable accompaniment of youth and beauty.

Lorraine learned rapidly. In three years she thrilled to more blood-curdling adventure than all the Bad Men in all the West could have furnished had they lived to be old and worked hard at being bad all their lives. For in that third year she worked her way enthusiastically through a sixteen-episode movie serial called "The Terror of the Range." She was past mistress of romance by that time. She knew her West.

It was just after the "Terror of the Range" was finished that a great revulsion in the management of this particular company stopped production with a stunning completeness that left actors and actresses feeling very much as if the studio roof had fallen upon them. Lorraine's West vanished. The little cow-town "set" was being torn down to make room for something else quite different. The cowboys appeared in tailored suits and drifted away. Lorraine went home to the Casa Grande, hating it more than ever she had hated it in her life.

Some one up-stairs was frying liver and onions, which was in flagrant defiance of Rule Four which mentioned cabbage, onions and fried fish as undesirable foodstuffs. Outside, the palm leaves were dripping in the night fog that had swept soggily in from the ocean. Her mother was trying to collect a gas bill from the dressmaker down the hall, who protested shrilly that she distinctly remembered having paid that gas bill once and had no intention of paying it twice.

Lorraine opened the door marked LANDLADY, and closed it with a slam intended to remind her mother that bickerings in the hall were less desirable than the odor of fried onions. She had often spoken to her mother about the vulgarity of arguing in public with the tenants, but her mother never seemed to see things as Lorraine saw them.

In the apartment sat a man who had been too frequent a visitor, as Lorraine judged him. He was an oldish man with the lines of failure in his face and on his lean form the sprightly clothing of youth. He had been a reporter, - was still, he maintained. But Lorraine suspected shrewdly that he scarcely made a living for himself, and that he was home-hunting in more ways than one when he came to visit her mother.

The affair had progressed appreciably in her absence, it would appear. He greeted her with, a fatherly "Hello, kiddie," and would have kissed her had Lorraine not evaded him skilfully.

Her mother came in then and complained intimately to the man, and declared that the dressmaker would have to pay that bill or have her gas turned off. He offered sympathy, assistance in the turning off of the gas, and a kiss which was perfectly audible to Lorraine in the next room. The affair had indeed progressed!

"L'raine, d'you know you've got a new papa?" her mother called out in the peculiar, chirpy tone she used when she was exuberantly happy. "I knew you'd be surprised!"

"I am," Lorraine agreed, pulling aside the cheap green portieres and looked in upon the two. Her tone was unenthusiastic. "A superfluous gift of doubtful value. I do not feel the need of a papa, thank you. If you want him for a husband, mother, that is entirely your own affair. I hope you'll be very happy."

"The kid don't want a papa; husbands are what means the most in her young life," chuckled the groom, restraining his bride when she would have risen from his knee.

"I hope you'll both be very happy indeed," said Lorraine gravely. "Now you won't mind, mother, when I tell you that I am going to dad's ranch in Idaho. I really meant it for a vacation, but since you won't be alone, I may stay with dad permanently. I'm leaving to-morrow or the next day - just as soon as I can pack my trunk and get a Pullman berth."

She did not wait to see the relief in her mother's face contradicting the expostulations on her lips. She went out to the telephone in the hall, remembered suddenly that her business would be overheard by half the tenants, and decided to use the public telephone in a hotel farther down the street. Her decision to go to her dad had been born with the words on her lips. But it was a lusty, full-voiced young decision, and it was growing at an amazing rate.

Of course she would go to her dad in Idaho! She was astonished that the idea had never before crystallized into action. Why should she feed her imagination upon a mimic West, when the great, glorious real West was there? What if her dad had not written a word for more than a year? He must be alive; they would surely have heard of his death, for she and Royal were his sole heirs, and his partner would have their address.

She walked fast and arrived at the telephone booth so breathless that she was compelled to wait a few minutes before she could call her number. She inquired about trains and rates to Echo, Idaho.

Echo, Idaho! While she waited for the information clerk to look it up the very words conjured visions of wide horizons and clean winds and high adventure. If she pictured Echo, Idaho, as being a replica of the "set" used in the movie serial, can you wonder? If she saw herself, the beloved queen of her father's cowboys, dashing into Echo, Idaho, on a crimply-maned broncho that pirouetted gaily before the post-office while handsome young men in chaps and spurs and "big four" Stetsons watched her yearningly, she was merely living mentally the only West that she knew.

From that beatific vision Lorraine floated into others more entrancing. All the hairbreadth escapes of the heroine of the movie serial were hers, adapted by her native logic to fit within the bounds of possibility, - though I must admit they bulged here and there and threatened to overlap and to encroach upon the impossible. Over the hills where her father's vast herds grazed, sleek and wild and long-horned and prone to stampede, galloped the Lorraine of Lorraine's dreams, on horses sure-footed and swift. With her galloped strong men whose faces limned the features of her favorite Western "lead."

That for all her three years of intermittent intimacy with a disillusioning world of mimicry, her dreams were pure romance, proved that Lorraine had still the unclouded innocence of her girlhood unspoiled.

## CHAPTER THREE

## REALITY IS WEIGHED AND FOUND WANTING

Still dreaming her dreams, still featuring herself as the star of many adventures, Lorraine followed the brakeman out of the dusty day coach and down the car steps to the platform of the place called Echo, Idaho. I can only guess at what she expected to find there in the person of a cattle-king father, but whatever it was she did not find it. No father, of any type whatever, came forward to claim her. In spite of her "Western" experience she looked about her for a taxi, or at least a street car. Even in the wilds of Western melodrama one could hear the clang of street-car gongs warning careless autoists off the track.

After the train had hooted and gone on around an absolutely uninteresting low hill of yellow barrenness dotted with stunted sage, it was the silence that first impressed Lorraine disagreeably. Echo, Idaho, was a very poor imitation of all the Western sets she had ever seen. True, it had the straggling row of square-fronted, one-story buildings, with hitch rails, but the signs painted across the fronts were absolutely common. Any director she had ever obeyed would have sent for his assistant director and would have used language which a lady must not listen to. Behind the store and the post-office and the blacksmith shop, on the brow of the low hill around whose point the train had disappeared, were houses with bay windows and porches absolutely out of keeping with the West. So far as Lorraine could see, there was not a log cabin in the whole place.

The hitch rails were empty, and there was not a cowboy in sight. Before the post-office a terribly grimy touring car stood with its running-boards loaded with canvas-covered suitcases. Three goggled, sunburned women in ugly khaki suits were disconsolately drinking soda water from bottles without straws, and a goggled, red-faced, angry-looking man was jerking impatiently at the hood of the machine. Lorraine and her suitcase apparently excited no interest whatever in Echo, Idaho.

The station agent was carrying two boxes of oranges and a crate of California cabbages in out of the sun, and a limp individual in blue gingham shirt and dirty overalls had shouldered the mail sack and was making his way across the dusty, rut-scored street to the post-office.

Two questions and two brief answers convinced her that the station agent did not know Britton Hunter, - which was strange, unless this happened to be a very new agent. Lorraine left him to his cabbages and followed the man with the mail sack.

At the post-office the anemic clerk came forward, eyeing her with admiring curiosity. Lorraine had seen anemic young men all her life, and the last three years had made her perfectly familiar with that look in a young man's eyes. She met it with impatient disfavor founded chiefly upon the young man's need of a decent hair-cut, a less flowery tie and a tailored suit. When he confessed that he did not know Mr. Britton Hunter by sight he ceased to exist so far as Lorraine was concerned. She decided that he also was new to the place and therefore perfectly useless to her.

The postmaster himself - Lorraine was cheered by his spectacles, his shirt sleeves, and his chin whiskers, which made him look the part - was better informed. He, too, eyed her curiously when she said "My father, Mr. Britton Hunter," but he made no comment on the relationship. He gave her a telegram and a letter from the General Delivery. The telegram, she suspected, was the one she had sent to her dad announcing the date of her arrival. The postmaster advised her to get a "livery rig" and drive out to the ranch, since it might be a week or two before any one came in from the Quirt. Lorraine thanked him graciously and departed for the livery stable.

The man in charge there chewed tobacco meditatively and told her that his teams were all out. If she was a mind to wait over a day or two, he said, he might maybe be able to make the trip. Lorraine took a long look at the structure which he indicated as the hotel.

"I think I'll walk," she said calmly.

"*Walk?*" The stableman stopped chewing and stared at her. "It's some consider'ble of a walk. It's all of eighteen mile - I dunno but twenty, time y'get to the house."

"I have frequently walked twenty-five or thirty miles. I am a member of the Sierra Club in Los Angeles. We seldom take hikes of less than twenty miles. If you will kindly tell me which road I must take -"

"There she is," the man stated flatly, and pointed across the railroad track to where a sandy road drew a yellowish line through the sage, evidently making for the hills showing hazily violet in the distance. Those hills formed the only break in the monotonous gray landscape, and Lorraine was glad that her journey would take her close to them.

"Thank you so much," she said coldly and returned to the station. In the small lavatory of the depot waiting room she exchanged her slippers for a pair of moderately low-heeled shoes which she had at the last minute of packing tucked into her suitcase, put a few extra articles into her rather smart traveling bag, left the suitcase in the telegraph office and started. Not another question would she ask of Echo, Idaho, which was flatter and more insipid than the drinking water in the tin "cooler" in the waiting room. The station agent stood with his hands on his hips and watched her cross the track and start down the road, pardonably astonished to see a young woman walk down a road that led only to the hills twenty miles away, carrying her luggage exactly as if her trip was a matter of a block or two at most.

The bag was rather heavy and as she went on it became heavier. She meant to carry it slung across her shoulder on a stick as soon as she was well away from the prying eyes of Echo's inhabitants. Later, if she felt tired, she could easily hide it behind a bush along the road and send one of her father's cowboys after it. The road was very dusty and carried the wind-blown traces of automobile tires. Some one would surely overtake her and give her a ride before she walked very far.

For the first half hour she believed that she was walking on level ground, but when she looked back there was no sign of any town behind her. Echo had disappeared as completely as if it had been swallowed. Even the unseemly bay-windowed houses on the hill had gone under. She walked for another half hour and saw only the gray sage stretching all around her. The hills looked farther away than when she started. Still, that beaten road must lead somewhere. Two hours later she began to wonder why this particular road should be so unending and so empty. Never in her life before had she walked for two hours without seeming to get anywhere, or without seeing any living human.

Both shoulders were sore from the weight of the bag on the stick, but the sagebushes looked so exactly alike that she feared she could not describe the particular spot where the cowboys would find her bag, wherefore she carried it still. She was beginning to change hands very often when the wind came.

Just where or how that wind sprang up she did not know. Suddenly it was whooping across the sage and flinging up clouds of dust from the road. To Lorraine, softened by years of southern California weather, it seemed to blow straight off an ice field, it was so cold.

After an interminable time which measured three hours on her watch, she came to an abrupt descent into a creek bed, down the middle of which the creek itself was flowing swiftly. Here the road forked, a rough, little-used trail keeping on up the creek, the better traveled road crossing and climbing the farther bank. Lorraine scarcely hesitated before she chose the main trail which crossed the creek.

From the creek the trail she followed kept climbing until Lorraine wondered if there would ever be a top. The wind whipped her narrow skirts and impeded her, tugged at her hat, tingled her nose and watered her eyes. But she kept on doggedly, disgustedly, the West, which she had seen through the glamour of swift-blooded Romance, sinking lower and lower in her estimation. Nothing but jack rabbits and little, twittery birds moved through the sage, though she watched hungrily for horsemen.

Quite suddenly the gray landscape glowed with a palpitating radiance, unreal, beautiful beyond expression. She stopped, turned to face the west and stared awestruck at one of those flaming sunsets which makes the desert land seem but a gateway into the ineffable glory beyond the earth. That the high-piled, gorgeous cloud-bank presaged a thunderstorm she never guessed; and that a thunderstorm may be a deadly, terrifying peril she never had quite believed. Her mother had told of people being struck by lightning, but Lorraine could not associate lightning with death, especially in the West, where men usually died by shooting, lynching, or by pitching over a cliff.

The wind hushed as suddenly as it had whooped. Warned by the twinkling lights far behind her - lights which must be the small part at last visible of Echo, Idaho - Lorraine went on. She had been walking steadily for four hours, and she must surely have come nearly twenty miles. If she ever reached the top of the hill, she believed that she would see her father's ranch just beyond.

The afterglow had deepened to dusk when she came at last to the highest point of that long grade. Far ahead loomed a cluster of square, black objects which must be the ranch buildings of the Quirt, and Lorraine's spirits lightened a little. What a surprise her father and all his cowboys would have when she walked in upon them! It was almost worth the walk, she told herself hearteningly. She hoped that dad had a good cook. He would wear a flour-sack apron, naturally, and would be tall and lean, or else very fat. He would be a comedy character, but she hoped he would not be the grouchy kind, which, though very funny when he rampages around on the screen, might be rather uncomfortable to meet when one is tired and hungry and out of sorts. But of course the crankiest of comedy cooks would be decently civil to *her*. Men always were, except directors who are paid for their incivility.

A hollow into which she walked in complete darkness and in silence, save the gurgling of another stream, hid from sight the shadowy semblance of houses and barns and sheds. Their disappearance slumped her spirits again, for without them she was no more than a solitary speck in the vast loneliness. Their actual nearness could not comfort her. She was seized with a reasonless, panicky fear that by the time she crossed the stream and climbed the hill beyond they would no longer be there where she had seen them. She was lifting her skirts to wade the creek when the click of hoofs striking against rocks sent her scurrying to cover in a senseless fear.

"I learned this act from the jack rabbits," she rallied herself shakily, when she was safely hidden behind a sagebush whose pungency made her horribly afraid that she might sneeze, which would be too ridiculous.

"Some of dad's cowboys, probably, but still they *may* be bandits."

If they were bandits they could scarcely be out banditting, for the two horsemen were talking in ordinary, conversational tones as they rode leisurely down to the ford. When they passed Lorraine, the horse nearest her shied against the other and was sworn at parenthetically for a fool. Against the skyline Lorraine saw the rider's form bulk squatty and ungraceful, reminding her of an actor whom she knew and did not like. It was that resemblance perhaps which held her quiet instead of following her first impulse to speak to them and ask them to carry her grip to the house.

The horses stopped with their forefeet in the water and drooped heads to drink thirstily. The riders continued their conversation.

"- and as I says time and again, they ain't big enough to fight the outfit, and the quicker they git out the less lead they'll carry under their hides when they do go. What they want to try an' hang on for, beats me. Why, it's like setting into a poker game with a five-cent piece! They ain't got my sympathy. I ain't got any use for a damn fool, no way yuh look at it."

"Well, there's the TJ - they been here a long while, and they ain't packin' any lead, and they ain't getting out."

"Well, say, lemme tell yuh something. The TJ'll git theirs and git it right. Drink all night, would yuh?" He swore long and fluently at his horse, spurred him through the shallows, and the two rode on up the hill, their voices still mingled in desultory argument, with now and then an oath rising clearly above the jumble of words.

They may have been law-abiding citizens riding home to families that were waiting supper for them, but Lorraine crept out from behind her sagebush, sneezing and thanking her imitation of the jack rabbits. Whoever they were, she was not sorry she had let them ride on. They might be her father's men, and they might have been very polite and chivalrous to her. But their voices and their manner of speaking had been rough; and it is one thing, Lorraine reflected, to mingle with made-up villains - even to be waylaid and kidnapped and tied to trees and threatened with death - but it is quite different to accost rough-speaking men in the dark when you know that they are not being rough to suit the director of the scene.

She was so absorbed in trying to construct a range war or something equally thrilling from the scrap of conversation she had heard that she reached the hilltop in what seemed a very few minutes of climbing. The sky was becoming overcast. Already the stars to the west were blotted out, and the absolute stillness of the atmosphere frightened her more than the big, dark wilderness itself. It seemed to her exactly as though the earth was holding its breath and waiting for something terrible to happen. The vague bulk of buildings was still some distance ahead, and when a rumble like the deepest notes of a pipe organ began to fill all the air, Lorraine thrust her grip under a bush and began to run, her soggy shoes squashing unpleasantly on the rough places in the road.

Lorraine had seen many stage storms and had thrilled ecstatically to the mimic lightning, knowing just how it was made. But when that huge blackness behind and to the left of her began to open and show a terrible brilliance within, and to close abruptly, leaving the world ink black, she was terrified. She wanted to hide as she had hidden from those two men; but from that stupendous monster, a real thunderstorm, sagebrush formed no protection whatever. She must reach the substantial shelter of buildings, the comforting presence of men and women.

She ran, and as she ran she wept aloud like a child and called for her father. The deep rumble grew louder, nearer. The revealed brilliance became swift sword-thrusts of blinding light that seemed to stab deep the earth. Lorraine ran awkwardly, her hands over her ears, crying out at each lightning flash, her voice drowned in the thunder that followed it close. Then, as she neared the somber group of buildings, the clouds above them split with a terrific, rending crash, and the whole place stood pitilessly revealed to her, as if a spotlight had been turned on. Lorraine stood aghast. The buildings were not buildings at all. They were rocks, great, black, forbidding boulders standing there on a narrow ridge, having a diabolic likeness to houses.

The human mind is wonderfully resilient, but readjustment comes slowly after a shock. Dumbly, refusing to admit the significance of what she had seen, Lorraine went forward. Not until she had reached and had touched the first grotesque caricature of habitation did she wholly grasp the fact that she was lost, and that shelter might be miles away. She stood and looked at the orderly group of boulders as the lightning intermittently revealed them. She saw where the road ran on, between two square-faced rocks. She would have to follow the road, for after all it must lead *somewhere*, - to her father's ranch, probably. She wondered irrelevantly why her mother had never mentioned these queer rocks, and she wondered vaguely if any of them had caves or ledges where she could be safe from the lightning.

She was on the point of stepping out into the road again when a horseman rode into sight between the two rocks. In the same instant of his appearance she heard the unmistakable crack of a gun, saw the rider jerk backward in the saddle, throw up one hand, - and then the darkness dropped between them.

Lorraine crouched behind a juniper bush close against the rock and waited. The next flash, came within a half-minute. It showed a man at the horse's head, holding it by the bridle. The horse was rearing. Lorraine tried to scream that the man on the ground would be trampled, but something went wrong with her voice, so that she could only whisper.

When the light came again the man who had been shot was not altogether on the ground. The other, working swiftly, had thrust the injured man's foot through the stirrup. Lorraine saw him stand back and lift his quirt to slash the horse across the rump. Even through the crash of thunder Lorraine heard the horse go past her down the hill, galloping furiously. When she could see again she glimpsed him running, while something bounced along on the ground beside him.

She saw the other man, with a dry branch in his hand, dragging it across the road where it ran between the two rocks. Then Lorraine Hunter, hardened to the sight of crimes committed for picture values only, realized sickeningly that she had just looked upon a real murder, - the cold-blooded killing of a man. She felt very sick. Queer little red sparks squirmed and danced before her eyes. She crumpled down quietly behind the juniper bush and did not know when the rain came, though it drenched her in the first two or three minutes of downpour.

## CHAPTER FOUR

## "SHE'S A GOOD GIRL WHEN SHE AIN'T CRAZY"

When the sun has been up just long enough to take the before-dawn chill from the air without having swallowed all the diamonds that spangle bush and twig and grass-blade after a night's soaking rain, it is good to ride over the hills of Idaho and feel oneself a king, - and never mind the crown and the scepter. Lone Morgan, riding early to the Sawtooth to see the foreman about getting a man for a few days to help replace a bridge carried fifty yards downstream by a local cloudburst, would not have changed places with a millionaire. The horse he rode was the horse he loved, the horse he talked to like a pal when they were by themselves. The ridge gave him a wide outlook to the four corners of the earth. Far to the north the Sawtooth range showed blue, the nearer mountains pansy purple where the pine trees stood, the foothills shaded delicately where canyons swept down to the gray plain. To the south was the sagebrush, a soft, gray-green carpet under the sun. The sky was blue, the clouds were handfuls of clean cotton floating lazily. Of the night's storm remained no trace save slippery mud when his horse struck a patch of clay, which was not often, and the packed sand still wet and soggy from the beating rain.

Rock City showed black and inhospitable even in the sunlight. The rock walls rose sheer, the roofs slanted rakishly, the signs scratched on the rock by facetious riders were pointless and inane. Lone picked his way through the crooked defile that was marked MAIN STREET on the corner of the first huge boulder and came abruptly into the road. Here he turned north and shook his horse into a trot.

A hundred yards or so down the slope beyond Rock City he pulled up short with a "What the hell!" that did not sound profane, but merely amazed. In the sodden road were the unmistakable footprints of a woman. Lone did not hesitate in naming the sex, for the wet sand held the imprint cleanly, daintily. Too shapely for a boy, too small for any one but a child or a woman with little feet, and with the point at the toes proclaiming the fashion of the towns, Lone guessed at once that she was a town girl, a stranger, probably, - and that she had passed since the rain; which meant since daylight.

He swung his horse and rode back, wondering where she could have spent the night. Halfway through Rock City the footprints ended abruptly, and Lone turned back, riding down the trail at a lope. She couldn't have gone far, he reasoned, and if she had been out all night in the rain, with no better shelter than Rock City afforded, she would need help, - "and lots of it, and pretty darn quick," he added to John Doe, which was the ambiguous name of his horse.

Half a mile farther on he overtook her. Rather, he sighted her in the trail, saw her duck in amongst the rocks and scattered brush of a small ravine, and spurred after her. It was precarious footing for his horse when he left the road, but John Doe was accustomed to that. He jumped boulders, shied around buckthorn, crashed through sagebrush and so brought the girl to bay against a wet bank, where she stood shivering. The terror in her face and her wide eyes would have made her famous in the movies. It made Lone afraid she was crazy.

Lone swung off and went up to her guardedly, not knowing just what an insane woman might do when cornered. "There, now, I'm not going to hurt yuh at all," he soothed. "I guess maybe you're lost. What made you run away from me when you saw me coming?"

Lorraine continued to stare at him.

"I'm going to the ranch, and if you'd like a ride, I'll lend you my horse. He'll be gentle if I lead him. It's a right smart walk from here." Lone smiled, meaning to reassure her.

"Are you the man I saw shoot that man and then fasten him to the stirrup of the saddle so the horse dragged him down the road? If you are, I - I -"

"No - oh, no, I'm not the man," Lone said gently. "I just now came from home. Better let me take you in to the ranch."

"I was going to the ranch - did you see him shoot that man and make the horse drag him - *make* the horse - he *slashed* that horse with the quirt - and he went tearing down the road dragging - it - it was - *horrible*!"

"Yes - yes, don't worry about it. We'll fix him. You come and get on John Doe and let me take you to the ranch. Come on - you're wet as a ducked pup."

"That man was just riding along - I saw him when it lightened. And he shot him - oh, can't you *do* something?"

"Yes, yes, they're after him right now. Here. Just put your foot in the stirrup - I'll help you up. Why, you're soaked!" Perseveringly Lone urged her to the horse. "You're soaking wet!" he exclaimed again.

"It rained," she muttered confusedly. "I thought it was the ranch - but they were rocks. Just rocks. Did you *see* him shoot that man? Why - why it shouldn't be allowed! He ought to be arrested right away - I'd have called a policeman but - isn't thunder and lightning just perfectly *awful*? And that horse - going down the road dragging -

"You'd better get some one to double for me in this scene," she said irrelevantly. "I - I don't know this horse, and if he starts running the boys might not catch him in time. It isn't safe, is it?"

"It's safe," said Lone pityingly. "You won't be dragged. You just get on and ride. I'll lead him. John Doe's gentle as a dog."

"Just straight riding?" Lorraine considered the matter gravely. "Wel-ll - but I saw a man dragged, once. He'd been shot first. It – it was awful!"

"I'll bet it was. How'd you come to be walking so far?"

Lorraine looked at him suspiciously. Lone thought her eyes were the most wonderful eyes - and the most terrible - that he had ever seen. Almond-shaped they were, the irises a clear, dark gray, the eyeballs blue-white like a healthy baby's. That was the wonder of them. But their glassy shine made them terrible. Her lids lifted in a sudden stare.

"You're not the man, are you? I - I think he was taller than you. And his hat was brown. He's a brute - a *beast*! To shoot a man just riding along - It rained," she added plaintively. "My bag is back there somewhere under a bush. I think I could find the bush - it was where a rabbit was sitting - but he's probably gone by this time. A rabbit," she told him impressively, "wouldn't sit out in the rain all night, would he? He'd get wet. And a rabbit would feel horrid when he was wet - such thick fur he never *would* get dried out. Where do they go when it rains? They have holes in the ground, don't they?"

"Yes. Sure, they do. I'll *show* you one, down the road here a little piece. Come on - it ain't far."

To see a rabbit hole in the ground, Lorraine consented to mount and ride while Lone walked beside her, agreeing with everything she said that needed agreement. When she had gone a few rods, however, she began to call him Charlie and to criticize the direction of the picture. They should not, she declared, mix murders and thunderstorms in the same scene. While the storm effect was perfectly *wonderful*, she thought it rather detracted from the killing. She did not believe in lumping big stuff together like that. Why not have the killing done by moonlight, and use the storm when the murderer was getting away, or something like that? And as for taking them out on location and making all those storm scenes without telling them in advance so that they could have dry clothes afterwards, she thought it a perfect outrage! If it were not for spoiling the picture, she would quit, she asserted indignantly. She thought the director had better go back to driving a laundry wagon, which was probably where he came from.

Lone agreed with her, even though he did not know what she was talking about. He walked as fast as he could, but even so he could not travel the six miles to the ranch very quickly. He could see that the girl was burning up with fever, and he could hear her voice growing husky, - could hear, too, the painful laboring of her breath. When she was not mumbling incoherent nonsense she was laughing hoarsely at the plight she was in, and after that she would hold both hands to her chest and moan in a way that made Lone grind his teeth.

When he lifted her off his horse at the foreman's cottage she was whispering things no one could understand. Three cowpunchers came running and hindered him a good deal in carrying her into the house, and the foreman's wife ran excitedly from one room to the other, asking questions and demanding that some one do something "for pity's sake, she may be dying for all you know, while you stand there gawping like fool-hens."

"She was out all night in the rain - got lost, somehow. She said she was coming here, so I brought her on. She's down with a cold, Mrs. Hawkins. Better take off them wet clothes and put hot blankets around her. And a poultice or something on her chest, I reckon." Lone turned to the door, stopped to roll a cigarette, and watched Mrs. Hawkins hurrying to Lorraine with a whisky toddy the cook had mixed for her.

"A sweat's awful good for a cold like she's got," he volunteered practically. "She's out of her head - or she was when I found her.

But I reckon that's mostly scare from being lost all night. Give her a good sweat, why don't you?" He reached the doorstep and then turned back to add, "She left a grip back somewhere along the road. I'll go hunt it up, I reckon."

He mounted John Doe and rode down to the corral, where two or three riders were killing time on various pretexts while they waited for details of Lone's adventure. Delirious young women of the silk-stocking class did not arrive at the Sawtooth every morning, and it was rumored already amongst the men that she was some looker, which naturally whetted their interest in her.

"I'll bet it's one of Bob's girls, come trailin' him up. Mebby another of them heart-ballum cases of Bob's," hazarded Pop Bridgers, who read nothing unless it was printed on pink paper, and who refused to believe that any good could come out of a city. "Ain't that right, Loney? Hain't she a heart-ballum girl of Bob's?"

From the saddle Lone stared down impassively at Pop and Pop's companions. "I don't know a thing about her," he stated emphatically. "She said she was coming to the ranch, and she was scared of the thunder and lightning. That's every word of sense I could get outa her. She ain't altogether ignorant - she knows how to climb on a horse, anyway, and she kicked about having to ride sideways on account of her skirts. She was plumb out of her head, and talked wild, but she handled her reins like a rider. And she never mentioned Bob, nor anybody else excepting some fellow she called Charlie. She thought I was him, but she only talked to me friendly. She didn't pull any love talk at all."

"Charlie?" Pop ruminated over a fresh quid of tobacco. "Charlie! Mebby Bob, he stakes himself to a different name now and then. There ain't any Charlie, except Charlie Werner; she wouldn't mean him, do yuh s'pose?"

"Charlie Werner? Hunh! Say, Pop, she ain't no squaw - is she, Loney?" Sid Sterling remonstrated.

"If I can read brands," Lone testified, "she's no girl of Bob's. She's a good, honest girl when she ain't crazy."

"And no good, honest girl who is not crazy could possibly be a girl of mine! Is that the idea, Lone?"

Lone turned unhurriedly and looked at young Bob Warfield standing in the stable door with his hands in his trousers pockets and his pipe in his mouth.

"That ain't the argument. Pop, here, was wondering if she was another heart-ballum girl of yours," Lone grinned unabashed. "I don't know such a hell of a lot about heart-balm ladies, Bob. I ain't a millionaire. I'm just making a guess at their brand - and it ain't the brand this little lady carries."

Bob removed one hand from his pocket and cuddled the bowl of his pipe. "If she's a woman, she's a heart-balmer if she gets the chance. They all are, down deep in their tricky hearts. There isn't a woman on earth that won't sell a man's soul out of his body if she happens to think it's worth her while - and she can get away with it. But don't for any sake call her *my* heart-balmer."

"That was Pop," drawled Lone. "It don't strike me as being any subject for you fellows to make remarks about, anyway," he advised Pop firmly. "She's a right nice little girl, and she's pretty darn sick." He touched John Doe with the spurs and rode away, stopping at the foreman's gate to finish his business with Hawkins. He was a conscientious young man, and since he had charge of Elk Spring camp, he set its interests above his own, which was more than some of the Sawtooth men would have done in his place.

Having reported the damage to the bridge and made his suggestions about the repairs, he touched up John Doe again and loped away on a purely personal matter, which had to do with finding the bag which the girl had told him was under a bush where a rabbit had been sitting.

If she had not been so very sick, Lone would have laughed at her naïve method of identifying the spot. But he was too sorry for her to be amused at the vagaries of her sick brain. He did not believe anything she had said, except that she had been coming to the ranch and had left her bag under a bush beside the road. It should not be difficult to find it, if he followed the road and watched closely the bushes on either side.

Until he reached the place where he had first sighted her, Lone rode swiftly, anxious to be through with the business and go his way. But when he came upon her footprints again, he pulled up and held John Doe to a walk, scanning each bush and boulder as he passed.

It seemed probable that she had left the grip at Rock City where she must have spent the night. She had spoken of being deceived into thinking the place was the Sawtooth ranch until she had come into it and found it "just rocks." Then, he reasoned, the storm had broken, and her fright had held her there. When daylight came she had either forgotten the bag or had left it deliberately.

At Rock City, then, Lone stopped to examine the base of every rock, even riding around those nearest the road. The girl, he guessed shrewdly, had not wandered off the main highway, else she would not have been able to find it again. Rock City was confusing unless one was perfectly familiar with its curious, winding lanes.

It was when he was riding slowly around the boulder marked "Palace Hotel, Rates Reasnible," that he came upon the place where a horse had stood, on the side best sheltered from the storm. Deep hoof marks closely overlapping, an over-turned stone here and there gave proof enough, and the rain-beaten soil that blurred the hoofprints farthest from the rock told him more. Lone backed away, dismounted, and, stepping carefully, went close. He could see no reason why a horse should have stood there with his head toward the road ten feet away, unless his rider was waiting for something - or some one. There were other boulders near which offered more shelter from rain.

Next the rock he discovered a boot track, evidently made when the rider dismounted. He thought of the wild statement of the girl about seeing some one shoot a man and wondered briefly if there could be a basis of truth in what she said. But the road showed no sign of a struggle, though there were, here and there, hoofprints half washed out with the rain.

Lone went back to his horse and rode on, still looking for the bag. His search was thorough and, being a keen-eyed young man, he discovered the place where Lorraine had crouched down by a rock. She must have stayed there all night, for the scuffed soil was dry where her body had rested, and her purse, caught in the juniper bush close by, was sodden with rain.

"The poor little kid!" he muttered, and with, a sudden impulse he turned and looked toward the rock behind which the horse had stood. Help had been that close, and she had not known it, unless -

"If anything happened there last night, she could have seen it from here," he decided, and immediately put the thought away from him.

"But nothing happened," he added, "unless maybe she saw him ride out and go on down the road. She was out of her head and just imagined things."

He slipped the soaked purse into his coat pocket, remounted and rode on slowly, looking for the grip and half-believing she had not been carrying one, but had dreamed it just as she had dreamed that a man had been shot.

He rode past the bag without seeing it, for Lorraine had thrust it far back under a stocky bush whose scraggly branches nearly touched the ground. So he came at last to the creek, swollen with the night's storm so that it was swift and dangerous. Lone was turning back when John Doe threw up his head, stared up the creek for a moment and whinnied shrilly. Lone stood in the stirrups and looked.

A blaze-faced horse was standing a short rifle-shot away, bridled and with an empty saddle. Whether he was tied or not Lone could not tell at that distance, but he knew the horse by its banged forelock and its white face and sorrel ears, and he knew the owner of the horse. He rode toward it slowly.

"Whoa, you rattle-headed fool," he admonished, when the horse snorted and backed a step or two as he approached. He saw the bridle-reins dangling, broken, where the horse had stepped on them in running. "Broke loose and run off again," he said, as he took down his rope and widened the loop. "I'll bet Thurman would sell you for a bent nickel, this morning."

The horse squatted and jumped when he cast the loop, and then stood quivering and snorting while Lone dismounted and started toward him. Ten steps from the horse Lone stopped short, staring. For down in the bushes on the farther side half lay, half hung the limp form of a man.

# CHAPTER FIVE

## A DEATH "BY ACCIDENT"

Lone Morgan was a Virginian by birth, though few of his acquaintances knew it. Lone never talked of himself except as his personal history touched a common interest with his fellows. But until he was seventeen he had lived very close to the center of one of the deadliest feuds of the Blue Ridge. That he had been neutral was merely an accident of birth, perhaps. And that he had not become involved in the quarrel that raged among his neighbors was the direct result of a genius for holding his tongue. He had attended the funerals of men shot down in their own dooryards, he had witnessed the trials of the killers. He had grown up with the settled conviction that other men's quarrels did not concern him so long as he was not directly involved, and that what did not concern him he had no right to discuss. If he stood aside and let violence stalk by unhindered, he was merely doing what he had been taught to do from the time he could walk. "Mind your own business and let other folks do the same," had been the family slogan in Lone's home. There had been nothing in Lone's later life to convince him that minding his own business was not a very good habit. It had grown to be second nature, - and it had made him a good man for the Sawtooth Cattle Company to have on its pay roll.

Just now Lone was stirred beyond his usual depth of emotion, and it was not altogether the sight of Fred Thurman's battered body that unnerved him. He wanted to believe that Thurman's death was purely an accident, - the accident it appeared. But Lorraine and the telltale hoofprints by the rock compelled him to believe that it was not an accident. He knew that if he examined carefully enough Fred Thurman's body he would find the mark of a bullet. He was tempted to look, and yet he did not want to know. It was no business of his; it would be foolish to let it become his business.

"He's too dead to care now how it happened - and it would only stir up trouble," he finally decided and turned his eyes away.

He pulled the twisted foot from the stirrup, left the body where it lay, and led the blaze-faced horse to a tree and tied it securely. He took off his coat and spread it over the head and shoulders of the dead man, weighted the edges with rocks and rode away.

Halfway up the hill he left the road and took a narrow trail through the sage, a short-cut that would save him a couple of miles.

The trail crossed the ridge half a mile beyond Rock City, dipping into the lower end of the small gulch where he had overtaken the girl. The place recalled with fresh vividness, her first words to him: "Are *you* the man I saw shoot that other man and fasten his foot in the stirrup?" Lone shivered and threw away the cigarette he had just lighted.

"My God, that girl mustn't tell that to any one else!" he exclaimed apprehensively. "No matter who she is or what she is, she mustn't tell that!"

"Hello! Who you talking to? I heard somebody talking -" The bushes parted above a low, rocky ledge and a face peered out, smiling good-humoredly. Lone started a little and pulled up.

"Oh, hello, Swan. I was just telling this horse of mine all I was going to do to him. Say, you're a chancey bird, Swan, yelling from the brush, like that. Some folks woulda taken a shot at you."

"Then they'd hit me, sure," Swan observed, letting himself down into the trail. He, too, was wet from his hat crown to his shoes, that squelched when he landed lightly on his toes. "Anybody would be ashamed to shoot at a mark so large as I am. I'd say they're poor shooters." And he added irrelevantly, as he held up a grayish pelt, "I got that coyote I been chasing for two weeks. He was sure smart. He had me guessing. But I made him guess some, maybe. He guessed wrong this time."

Lone's eyes narrowed while he looked Swan over. "You must have been out all night," he said. "You're crazier about hunting than I am."

"Wet bushes," Swan corrected carelessly. "I been tramping since daylight. It's my work to hunt, like it's your work to ride." He had swung into the trail ahead of John Doe and was walking with long strides, - the tallest, straightest, limberest young Swede in all the country. He had the bluest eyes, the readiest smile, the healthiest color, the sunniest hair and disposition the Sawtooth country had seen for many a day. He had homesteaded an eighty-acre claim on the south side of Bear Top and had by that means gained possession of two living springs and the only accessible portion of Wilder Creek where it crossed the meadow called Skyline before it plunged into a gulch too narrow for cattle to water with any safety.

The Sawtooth Cattle Company had for years "covered" that eighty-acre patch of government land, never dreaming that any one would ever file on it. Swan Vjolmar was there and had his log cabin roofed and ready for the door and windows before the Sawtooth discovered his presence. Now, nearly a year afterwards, he was accepted in a tolerant, half-friendly spirit. He had not objected to the Sawtooth cattle which still watered at Skyline Meadow. He was a "Government hunter" and he had killed many coyotes and lynx and even a mountain lion or two. Lone wondered sometimes what the Sawtooth meant to do about the Swede, but so far the Sawtooth seemed inclined to do nothing at all, evidently thinking his war on animal pests more than atoned for his effrontery in taking Skyline as a homestead. When he had proven up on his claim they would probably buy him out and have the water still.

"Well, what do you know?" Swan turned his head to inquire abruptly. "You're pretty quiet."

Lone roused himself. "Fred Thurman's been dragged to death by that damned flighty horse of his," he said. "I found him in the brush this side of Granite Creek. Had his foot caught in the stirrup. I thought I'd best leave him there till the coroner can view him."

Swan stopped short in the trail and turned facing Lone. "Last night my dog Yack whines to go out. He went and sat in a place where he looks down on the walley, and he howled for half an hour. I said then that somebody in the walley has died. That dog is something queer about it. He knows things."

"I'm going to the Sawtooth," Lone told him. "I can telephone to the coroner from there. Anybody at Thurman's place, do you know?"

Swan shook his head and started again down the winding, steep trail. "I don't hunt over that way for maybe a week. That's too bad he's killed. I like Fred Thurman. He's a fine man, you bet."

"He was," said Lone soberly. "It's a damn shame he had to go - like that."

Swan glanced back at him, studied Lone's face for an instant and turned into a tributary gully where a stream trickled down over water-worn rocks. "Here I leave you," he volunteered, as Lone came abreast of him. "A coyote's crossed up there, and I maybe find his tracks. I could go do chores for Fred Thurman if nobody's there. Should I do that? What you say, Lone?"

"You might drift around by there if it ain't too much out of your way, and see if he's got a man on the ranch," Lone suggested. "But you better not touch anything in the house, Swan. The coroner'll likely appoint somebody to look around and see if he's got any folks to send his stuff to. Just feed any stock that's kept up, if nobody's there."

"All right," Swan agreed readily. "I'll do that, Lone. Good-by."

Lone nodded and watched him climb the steep slope of the gulch on the side toward Thurman's ranch. Swan climbed swiftly, seeming to take no thought of where he put his feet, yet never once slipping or slowing. In two minutes he was out of sight, and Lone rode on moodily, trying not to think of Fred Thurman, trying to shut from his mind the things that wild-eyed, hoarse-voiced girl had told him.

"Lone, you mind your own business," he advised himself once. "You don't know anything that's going to do any one any good, and what you don't know there's no good guessing. But that girl - she mustn't talk like that!"

Of Swan he scarcely gave a thought after the Swede had disappeared, yet Swan was worth a thought or two, even from a man who was bent on minding his own business. Swan had no sooner climbed the gulch toward Thurman's claim than he proceeded to descend rather carefully to the bottom again, walk along on the rocks for some distance and climb to the ridge whose farther slope led down to Granite Creek. He did not follow the trail, but struck straight across an outcropping ledge, descended to Granite Creek and strode along next the hill where the soil was gravelly and barren. When he had gone some distance, he sat down and took from under his coat two huge, crudely made moccasins of coyote skin. These he pulled on over his shoes, tied them around his ankles and went on, still keeping close under the hill.

He reached the place where Fred Thurman lay, stood well away from the body and studied every detail closely. Then, stepping carefully on trampled brush and rocks, he approached and cautiously lifted Lone's coat. It was not a pretty sight, but Swan's interest held him there for perhaps ten minutes, his eyes leaving the body only when the blaze-faced horse moved. Then Swan would look up quickly at the horse, seem reassured when he saw that the animal was not watching anything at a distance, and return to his curious task. Finally he drew the coat back over the head and shoulders, placed each stone exactly as he had found it and went up to the horse, examining the saddle rather closely. After that he retreated as carefully as he had approached. When he had gone half a mile or so upstream he found a place where he could wash his hands without wetting his moccasins, returned to the rocky hillside and took off the clumsy footgear and stowed them away under his coat. Then with long strides that covered the ground as fast as a horse could do without loping, Swan headed as straight as might be for the Thurman ranch.

About noon Swan approached the crowd of men and a few women who stood at a little distance and whispered together, with their faces averted from the body around which the men stood grouped. The news had spread as such news will, even in a country so sparsely settled as the Sawtooth. Swan counted forty men, - he did not bother with the women. Fred Thurman had been known to every one of them. Some one had spread a piece of canvas over the corpse, and Swan did not go very near. The blaze-faced horse had been led farther away and tied to a cottonwood, where some one had thrown down a bundle of hay. The Sawtooth country was rather punctilious in its duty toward the law, and it was generally believed that the coroner would want to see the horse that had caused the tragedy.

Half an hour after Swan arrived, the coroner came in a machine, and with him came the sheriff. The coroner, an important little man, examined the body, the horse and the saddle, and there was the usual formula of swearing in a jury. The inquest was rather short, since there was only one witness to testify, and Lone merely told how he had discovered the horse there by the creek, and that the body had not been moved from where he found it.

Swan went over to where Lone, anxious to get away from the place, was untying his horse after the jury had officially named the death an accident.

"I guess those horses could be turned loose," he began without prelude. "What you think, Lone? I been to Thurman's ranch, and I don't find anybody. Some horses in a corral, and pigs in a pen, and chickens. I guess Thurman was living alone. Should I tell the coroner that?"

"I dunno," Lone replied shortly. "You might speak to the sheriff. I reckon he's the man to take charge of things."

"It's bad business, getting killed," Swan said vaguely. "It makes me feel damn sorry when I go to that ranch. There's the horses waiting for breakfast - and Thurman, he's dead over here and can't feed his pigs and his chickens. It's a white cat over there that comes to meet me and rubs my leg and purrs like it's lonesome. That's a nice ranch he's got, too. Now what becomes of that ranch? What you think, Lone?"

"Hell, how should I know?" Lone scowled at him from the saddle and rode away, leaving Swan standing there staring after him. He turned away to find the sheriff and almost collided with Brit Hunter, who was glancing speculatively from him to Lone Morgan. Swan stopped and put out his hand to shake.

"Lone says I should tell the sheriff I could look after Fred Thurman's ranch. What you think, Mr. Hunter?"

"Good idea, I guess. Somebody'll have to. They can't -" He checked himself. "You got a horse? I'll ride over with yuh, maybe."

"I got legs," Swan returned laconically. "They don't get scared, Mr. Hunter, and maybe kill me sometime. You could tell the sheriff I'm government hunter and honest man, and I take good care of things. You could do that, please?"

"Sure," said Brit and rode over to where the sheriff was standing.

The sheriff listened, nodded, beckoned to Swan. "The court'll have to settle up the estate and find his heirs, if he's got any. But you look after things - what's your name? Vjolmar - how yuh spell it? I'll swear you in as a deputy. Good Lord, you're a husky son-of-a-gun!" The sheriff's eyes went up to Swan's hat crown, descended to his shoulders and lingered there admiringly for a moment, traveled down his flat, hard-muscled body and his straight legs. "I'll bet you could put up some fight, if you had to," he commented.

Swan grinned good-humoredly, glanced conscience-stricken at the covered figure on the ground and straightened his face decorously.

"I could lick you good," he admitted in a stage whisper. "I'm a son-off-a-gun all right - only I don't never get mad at somebody."

Brit Hunter smiled at that, it was so like Swan Vjolmar. But when they were halfway to Thurman's ranch - Brit on horseback and Swan striding easily along beside him, leading the blaze-faced horse, he glanced down at Swan's face and wondered if Swan had not lied a little.

"What's on your mind, Swan?" he asked abruptly.

Swan started and looked up at him, glanced at the empty hills on either side, and stopped still in the trail.

"Mr. Hunter, you been longer in the country than I have been. You seen some good riding, I bet. Maybe you see some men ride backwards on a horse?"

Brit looked at him uncomprehendingly. "Backwards?"

Swan led up the blaze-faced horse and pointed to the right stirrup. "Spurs would scratch like that if you jerk your foot, maybe. You're a good rider, Mr. Hunter, you can tell. That's a right stirrup, ain't it? Fred Thurman, he's got his left foot twist around, all broke from jerking in his stirrup. Left foot in right stirrup -" He pushed back his hat and rumpled his yellow hair, looking up into Brit's face inquiringly. "Left foot in right stirrup is riding backwards. That's a damn good rider to ride like that - what you think, Mr. Hunter?"

## CHAPTER SIX

## LONE ADVISES SILENCE

Twice in the next week Lone found an excuse for riding over to the Sawtooth. During his first visit, the foreman's wife told him that the young lady was still too sick to talk much. The second time he went, Pop Bridgers spied him first and cackled over his coming to see the girl. Lone grinned and dissembled as best he could, knowing that Pop Bridgers fed his imagination upon denials and argument and remonstrance and was likely to build gossip that might spread beyond the Sawtooth. Wherefore he did not go near the foreman's house that day, but contented himself with gathering from Pop's talk that the girl was still there.

After that he rode here and there, wherever he would be likely to meet a Sawtooth rider, and so at last he came upon Al Woodruff loping along the crest of Juniper Ridge. Al at first displayed no intention of stopping, but pulled up when he saw John Doe slowing down significantly. Lone would have preferred a chat with some one else, for this was a sharp-eyed, sharp-tongued man; but Al Woodruff stayed at the ranch and would know all the news, and even though he might give it an ill-natured twist, Lone would at least know what was going on. Al hailed him with a laughing epithet.

"Say, you sure enough played hell all around, bringin' Brit Hunter's girl to the Sawtooth!" he began, chuckling as if he had some secret joke. "Where'd you pick her up, Lone? She claims you found her at Rock City. That right?"

"No, it ain't right," Lone denied promptly, his dark eyes meeting Al's glance steadily. "I found her in that gulch away this side. She was in amongst the rocks where she was trying to keep outa the rain. Brit Hunter's girl, is she? She told me she was going to the Sawtooth. She'd have made it, too, if it hadn't been for the storm. She got as far as the gulch, and the lightning scared her from going any farther." He offered Al his tobacco sack and fumbled for a match. "I never knew Brit Hunter had a girl."

"Nor me," Al said and sifted tobacco into a cigarette paper. "Bob, he drove her over there yesterday. Took him close to all day to make the trip - and Bob, he claims to hate women!"

"So would I, if I'd got stung for fifty thousand. She ain't that kind. She's a nice girl, far as I could tell. She got well, all right, did she?"

"Yeah - only she was still coughing some when she left the ranch. She like to of had pneumonia, I guess. Queer how she claimed she spent the night in Rock City, ain't it?"

"No," Lone answered judicially, "I don't know as it's so queer. She never realized how far she'd walked, I reckon. She was plumb crazy when I found her. You couldn't take any stock in what she said. Say, you didn't see that bay I was halter-breaking, did yuh, Al? He jumped the fence and got away on me, day before yesterday. I'd like to catch him up again. He'll make a good horse."

Al had not seen the bay, and the talk tapered off desultorily to a final "So-long, see yuh later." Lone rode on, careful not to look back. So she was Brit Hunter's girl! Lone whistled softly to himself while he studied this new angle of the problem, - for a problem he was beginning to consider it. She was Brit Hunter's girl, and she had told them at the Sawtooth that she had spent the night at Rock City. He wondered how much else she had told; how much she remembered of what she had told him.

He reached into his coat pocket and pulled out a round leather purse with a chain handle. It was soiled and shrunken with its wetting, and the clasp had flecks of rust upon it. What it contained Lone did not know. Virginia had taught him that a man must not be curious about the personal belongings of a woman. Now he turned the purse over, tried to rub out the stiffness of the leather, and smiled a little as he dropped it back into his pocket.

"I've got my calling card," he said softly to John Doe. "I reckon I had the right hunch when I didn't turn it over to Mrs. Hawkins. I'll ask her again about that grip she said she hid under a bush. I never heard about any of the boys finding it."

His thoughts returned to Al Woodruff and stopped there. Determined still to attend strictly to his own affairs, his thoughts persisted in playing truant and in straying to a subject he much preferred not to think of at all. Why should Al Woodruff be interested in the exact spot where Brit Hunter's daughter had spent the night of the storm? Why should Lone instinctively discount her statement and lie whole-heartedly about it?

"Now if Al catches me up in that, he'll think I know a lot I don't know, or else -" He halted his thoughts there, for that, too, was a forbidden subject.

Forbidden subjects are like other forbidden things: they have a way of making themselves very conspicuous. Lone was heading for the Quirt ranch by the most direct route, fearing, perhaps, that if he waited he would lose his nerve and would not go at all. Yet it was important that he should go; he must return the girl's purse!

The most direct route to the Quirt took him down Juniper Ridge and across Granite Creek near the Thurman ranch. Indeed, if he followed the trail up Granite Creek and across the hilly country to Quirt Creek, he must pass within fifty yards of the Thurman cabin. Lone's time was limited, yet he took the direct route rather reluctantly. He did not want to be reminded too sharply of Fred Thurman as a man who had lived his life in his own way and had died so horribly.

"Well, he didn't have it coming to him - but it's done and over with, now, so it's no use thinking about it," he reflected, when the roofs of the Thurman ranch buildings began to show now and then through the thin ranks of the cottonwoods along the creek.

But his face sobered as he rode along. It seemed to him that the sleepy little meadows, the quiet murmuring of the creek, even the soft rustling of the cottonwood leaves breathed a new loneliness, an emptiness where the man who had called this place home, who had clung to it in the face of opposition that was growing into open warfare, had lived and had left life suddenly - unwarrantably, Lone knew in his heart. It might be of no use to think about it, but the vivid memory of Fred Thurman was with him when he rode up the trail to the stable and the small corrals. He had to think, whether he would or no.

At the corral he came unexpectedly in sight of the Swede, who grinned a guileless welcome and came toward him, so that Lone could not ride on unless he would advertise his dislike of the place. John Doe, plainly glad to find an excuse to stop, slowed and came to where Swan waited by the gate.

"By golly, this is lonesome here," Swan complained, heaving a great sigh. "That judge don't get busy pretty quick, I'm maybe jumping my job. Lone, what you think? You believe in ghosts?"

"Naw. What's on your chest, Swan?" Lone slipped sidewise in the saddle, resting his muscles. "You been seeing things?"

"No - I don't be seeing things, Lone. But sometimes I been - like I *feel* something." He stared at Lone questioningly. "What you think, Lone, if you be sitting down eating your supper, maybe, and you feel something say words in your brain? Like you know something talks to you and then quits."

Lone gave Swan a long, measuring look, and Swan laughed uneasily.

"That sounds crazy. But it's true, what something tells me in my brain. I go and look, and by golly, it's there just like the words tell me."

Lone straightened in the saddle. "You better come clean, Swan, and tell the whole thing. What was it? Don't talk in circles. What words did you feel - in your brain?" In spite of himself, Lone felt as he had when the girl had talked to him and called him Charlie.

Swan closed the gate behind him with steady hands. His lips were pressed firmly together, as if he had definitely made up his mind to something. Lone was impressed somehow with Swan's perfect control of his speech, his thoughts, his actions. But he was puzzled rather than anything else, and when Swan turned, facing him, Lone's bewilderment did not lessen.

"I'll tell you. It's when I'm sitting down to eat my supper. I'm just reaching out my hand like this, to get my coffee. And something says in my head, 'It's a lie. I don't ride backwards. Go look at my saddle. There's blood - ' And that's all. It's like the words go far away so I can't hear any more. So I eat my supper, and then I get the lantern and I go look. You come with me, Lone. I'll show you."

Without a word Lone dismounted and followed Swan into a small shed beside the stable, where a worn stock saddle hung suspended from a crosspiece, a rawhide string looped over the horn. Lone did not ask whose saddle it was, nor did Swan name the owner. There was no need.

Swan took the saddle and swung it around so that the right side was toward them. It was what is called a full-stamped saddle, with the popular wild-rose design on skirts and cantle. Much hard use and occasional oilings had darkened the leather to a rich, red brown, marred with old scars and scratches and the stains of many storms.

"Blood is hard to find when it's raining all night," Swan observed, speaking low as one does in the presence of death. "But if somebody is bleeding and falls off a horse slow, and catches hold of things and tries like hell to hang on -" He lifted the small flap that covered the cinch ring and revealed a reddish, flaked stain. Phlegmatically he wetted his finger tip on his tongue, rubbed the stain and held up his finger for Lone to see. "That's a damn funny place for blood, when a man is dragging on the ground," he commented drily. "And something else is damn funny, Lone."

He lifted the wooden stirrup and touched with his finger the rowel marks. "That is on the front part," he said. "I could swear in court that Fred's left foot was twisted - that's damn funny, Lone. I don't see men ride backwards, much."

Lone turned on him and struck the stirrup from his hand. "I think you better forget it," he said fiercely. "He's dead - it can't help him any to -" He stopped and pulled himself together. "Swan, you take a fool's advice and don't tell anybody else about feeling words talk in your head. They'll have you in the bug-house at Blackfoot, sure as you live." He looked at the saddle, hesitated, looked again at Swan, who was watching him. "That blood most likely got there when Fred was packing a deer in from the hills. And marks on them old oxbow stirrups don't mean a damn thing but the need of a new pair, maybe." He forced a laugh and stepped outside the shed. "Just shows you, Swan, that imagination and being alone all the time can raise Cain with a fellow. You want to watch yourself."

Swan followed him out, closing the door carefully behind him. "By golly, I'm watching out now," he assented thoughtfully. "You don't tell anybody, Lone."

"No, I won't tell anybody - and I'd advise you not to," Lone repeated grimly. "Just keep those thoughts outa your head, Swan. They're bad medicine."

He mounted John Doe and rode away, his eyes downcast, his quirt slapping absently the weeds along the trail. It was not his business, and yet - Lone shook himself together and put John Doe into a lope. He had warned Swan, and he could do no more.

Halfway to the Quirt he met Lorraine riding along the trail. She would have passed him with no sign of recognition, but Lone lifted his hat and stopped. Lorraine looked at him, rode on a few steps and turned. "Did you wish to speak about something?" she asked impersonally.

Lone felt the flush in his cheeks, which angered him to the point of speaking curtly. "Yes. I found your purse where you dropped it that night you were lost. I was bringing it over to you. My name's Morgan. I'm the man that found you and took you in to the ranch."

"Oh." Lorraine looked at him steadily. "You're the one they call Loney?"

"When they're feeling good toward me. I'm Lone Morgan. I went back to find your grip - you said you left it under a bush, but the world's plumb full of bushes. I found your purse, though."

"Thank you so much. I must have been an awful nuisance, but I was so scared - and things were terribly mixed in my mind. I didn't even have sense enough to tell you what ranch I was trying to find, did I? So you took me to the wrong one, and I was a week there before I found it out. And then they were perfectly lovely about it and brought me - home." She turned the purse over and over in her hands, looking at it without much interest. She seemed in no hurry to ride on, which gave Lone courage.

"There's something I'd like to say," he began, groping for words that would make his meaning plain without telling too much. "I hope you won't mind my telling you. You were kinda out of your head when I found you, and you said something about seeing a man shot and -"

"Oh!" Lorraine looked up at him, looked through him, he thought, with those brilliant eyes of hers. "Then I did tell -"

"I just wanted to say," Lone interrupted her, "that I knew all the time it was just a nightmare. I never mentioned it to anybody, and you'll forget all about it, I hope. You didn't tell any one else, did you?"

He looked up at her again and found her studying him curiously. "You're not the man I saw," she said, as if she were satisfying herself on that point. "I've wondered since - but I was sure, too, that I had seen it. Why mustn't I tell any one?"

Lone did not reply at once. The girl's eyes were disconcertingly direct, her voice and her manner disturbed him with their judicial calmness, so at variance with the wildness he remembered.

"Well, it's hard to explain," he said at last. "You're strange to this country, and you don't know all the ins and outs of - things. It wouldn't do any good to you or anybody else, and it might do a lot of harm." His eyes nicked her face with a wistful glance. "You don't know me - I really haven't got any right to ask or expect you to trust me. But I wish you would, to the extent of forgetting that you saw - or thought you saw - anything that night in Rock City."

Lorraine shivered and covered her eyes swiftly with one hand. His words had brought back too sharply that scene. But she shook off the emotion and faced him again.

"I saw a man murdered," she cried. "I wasn't sure afterwards; sometimes I thought I had dreamed it. But I was sure I saw it. I saw the horse go by, running - and you want me to keep still about that? What harm could it do to tell? Perhaps it's true - perhaps I did see it all. I might think you were trying to cover up something - only, you're not the man I saw - or thought I saw."

"No, of course I'm not. You dreamed the whole thing, and the way you talked to me was so wild, folks would say you're crazy if they heard you tell it. You're a stranger here, Miss Hunter, and - your father is not as popular in this country as he might be. He's got enemies that would be glad of the chance to stir up trouble for him. You - just dreamed all that. I'm asking you to forget a bad dream, that's all, and not go telling it to other folks."

For some time Lorraine did not answer. The horses conversed with sundry nose-rubbings, nibbled idly at convenient brush tips, and wondered no doubt why their riders were so silent. Lone tried to think of some stronger argument, some appeal that would reach the girl without frightening her or causing her to distrust him. But he did not know what more he could say without telling her what must not be told.

"Just how would it make trouble for my father?" Lorraine asked at last. "I can't believe you'd ask me to help cover up a crime, but it seems hard to believe that a nightmare would cause any great commotion. And why is my father unpopular?"

"Well, you don't know this country," Lone parried inexpertly. "It's all right in some ways, and in some ways it could be a lot improved. Folks haven't got much to talk about. They go around gabbling their heads off about every little thing, and adding onto it until you can't recognize your own remarks after they've been peddled for a week. You've maybe seen places like that."

"Oh, yes." Lorraine's eyes lighted with a smile. "Take a movie studio, for instance."

"Yes. Well, you being a stranger, you would get all the worst of it. I just thought I'd tell you; I'd hate to see you misunderstood by folks around here. I - I feel kinda responsible for you; I'm the one that found you."

Lorraine's eyes twinkled. "Well, I'm glad to know one person in the country who doesn't gabble his head off. You haven't answered any of my questions, and you've made me feel as if you'd found a dangerous, wild woman that morning. It isn't very flattering, but I think you're honest, anyway."

Lone smiled for the first time, and she found his smile pleasant. "I'm no angel," he disclaimed modestly, "and most folks think I could be improved on a whole lot. But I'm honest in one way. I'm thinking about what's best for you, this time."

"I'm terribly grateful," Lorraine laughed. "I shall take great care not to go all around the country telling people my dreams. I can see that it wouldn't make me awfully popular." Then she sobered. "Mr. Morgan, that was a *horrible* kind of - nightmare. Why, even last night I woke up shivering, just imagining it all over again."

"It was sure horrible the way you talked about it," Lone assured her. "It's because you were sick, I reckon. I wish you'd tell me as close as you can where you left that grip of yours. You said it was under a bush where a rabbit was sitting. I'd like to find the grip - but I'm afraid that rabbit has done moved!"

"Oh, Mr. Warfield and I found it, thank you. The rabbit had moved, but I sort of remembered how the road had looked along there, and we hunted until we discovered the place. Dad has driven in after my other luggage to-day - and I believe I must be getting home. I was only out for a little ride."

She thanked him again for the trouble he had taken and rode away. Lone turned off the trail and, picking his way around rough outcroppings of rock, and across unexpected little gullies, headed straight for the ford across Granite Creek and home. Brit Hunter's girl, he was thinking, was even nicer than he had pictured her. And that she could believe in the nightmare was a vast relief.

## CHAPTER SEVEN

## THE MAN AT WHISPER

Brit Hunter finished washing the breakfast dishes and put a stick of wood into the broken old cook-stove that had served him and Frank for fifteen years and was feeling its age. Lorraine's breakfast was in the oven, keeping warm. Brit looked in, tested the heat with his gnarled hand to make sure that the sour-dough biscuits would not be dried to crusts, and closed the door upon them and the bacon and fried potatoes. Frank Johnson had the horses saddled and it was time to go, yet Brit lingered, uneasily conscious that his habitation was lacking in many things which a beautiful young woman might consider absolute necessities. He had seen in Lorraine's eyes, as they glanced here and there about the grimy walls, a certain disparagement of her surroundings. The look had made him wince, though he could not quite decide what it was that displeased her. Maybe she wanted lace curtains, or something.

He set the four chairs in a row against the wall, swept up the bits of bark and ashes beside the stove, made sure that the water bucket was standing full on its bench beside the door, sent another critical glance around the room, and tiptoed over to the dish cupboard and let down the flowered calico curtain that had been looped up over a nail for convenience. The sun sent a bright, wide bar of yellow light across the room to rest on the shelf behind the stove where stood the salt can, the soda, the teapot, a box of matches and two pepper cans, one empty and the other full. Brit always meant to throw out that empty pepper can and always neglected to do so. Just now he remembered picking up the empty one and shaking it over the potatoes futilely and then changing it for the full one. But he did not take it away; in the wilderness one learns to save useless things in the faint hope that some day they may become useful. The shelves were cluttered with fit companions to that empty pepper can. Brit thought that he would have "cleaned out" had he known that Lorraine was coming. Since she was here, it scarcely seemed worth while.

He walked on his boot-toes to the door of the second room of the cabin, listened there for a minute, heard no sound and took a tablet and pencil off another shelf littered with useless things. The note which he wrote painstakingly, lest she might think him lacking in education, he laid upon the table beside Lorraine's plate; then went out, closing the door behind him as quietly as a squeaking door can be made to close.

Lorraine, in the other room, heard the squeak and sat up. Her wrist watch, on the chair beside her bed, said that it was fifteen minutes past six, which she considered an unearthly hour for rising. She pulled up the covers and tried to sleep again. The day would be long enough, at best. There was nothing to do, unless she took that queer old horse with withers like the breastbone of a lean Christmas turkey and hips that reminded her of the little roofs over dormer windows, and went for a ride. And if she did that, there was nowhere to go and nothing to do when she arrived there.

In a very few days Lorraine had exhausted the sights of Quirt Creek and vicinity. If she rode south she would eventually come to the top of a hill whence she could look down upon further stretches of barrenness. If she rode east she would come eventually to the road along which she had walked from Echo, Idaho. Lorraine had had enough of that road. If she went north she would - well, she would not meet Mr. Lone Morgan again, for she had tried it twice, and had turned back because there seemed no end to the trail twisting through the sage and rocks. West she had not gone, but she had no doubt that it would be the same dreary monotony of dull gray landscape.

Monotony of landscape was one thing which Lorraine could not endure, unless it had a foreground of riders hurtling here and there, and of perspiring men around a camera tripod. At the Sawtooth ranch, after she was able to be up, she had seen cowboys, but they had lacked the dash and the picturesque costuming of the West she knew. They were mostly commonplace young men, jogging past the house on horseback, or loitering down by the corrals. They had offered absolutely no interest or "color" to the place, and the owner's son, Bob Warfield, had driven her over to the Quirt in a Ford and had seemed exactly like any other big, good-looking young man who thought well of himself. Lorraine was not susceptible to mere good looks, three years with the "movies" having disillusioned her quite thoroughly. Too many young men of Bob Warfield's general type had attempted to make love to her - lightly and not too well - for Lorraine to be greatly impressed.

She yawned, looked at her watch again, found that she had spent exactly six minutes in meditating upon her immediate surroundings, and fell to wondering why it was that the real West was so terribly commonplace. Why, yesterday she had been brought to such a pass of sheer loneliness that she had actually been driven to reading an old horse-doctor book! She had learned the symptoms of epizooetic - whatever that was - and poll-evil and stringhalt, and had gone from that to making a shopping tour through a Montgomery Ward catalogue. There was nothing else in the house to read, except a half dozen old copies of the *Boise News*.

There was nothing to do, nothing to see, no one to talk to. Her dad and the big, heavy-set man whom he called Frank, seemed uncomfortably aware of their deficiencies and were pitiably anxious to make her feel welcome, - and failed. They called her "Raine." The other two men did not call her anything at all. They were both sandy-complexioned and they both chewed tobacco quite noticeably, and when they sat down in their shirt sleeves to eat, Lorraine had seen irregular humps in their hip pockets which must be six-guns; though why they should carry them in their pockets instead of in holster belts buckled properly around their bodies and sagging savagely down at one side and swinging ferociously when they walked, Lorraine could not imagine. They did not wear chaps, either, and their spurs were just spurs, without so much as a silver concho anywhere. Cowboys in overalls and blue gingham shirts and faded old coats whose lapels lay in wrinkles and whose pockets were torn down at the corners! If Lorraine had not been positive that this was actually a cattle ranch in Idaho, she never would have believed that they were anything but day laborers.

"It's a comedy part for the cattle-queen's daughter," she admitted, putting out a hand to stroke the lean, gray cat that jumped upon her bed from the open window. "Ket, it's a *scream*! I'll take my West before the camera, thank you; or I would, if I hadn't jumped right into the middle of this trick West before I knew what I was doing. Ket, what do you do to pass away the time? I don't see how you can have the nerve to live in an empty space like this and purr!"

She got up then, looked into the kitchen and saw the paper on the table. This was new and vaguely promised some sort of break in the deadly monotony which she saw stretching endlessly before her. Carrying the nameless cat in her arms, Lorraine went in her bare feet across the grimy, bare floor to the table and picked up the note. It read simply:

> "Your brekfast is in the oven we wont be back till dark maby. Don't leave the ranch today. Yr loveing father."

Lorraine hugged the cat so violently that she choked off a purr in the middle. "'Don't leave the ranch to-day!' Ket, I believe it's going to be dangerous or something, after all."

She dressed quickly and went outside into the sunlight, the cat at her heels, the thrill of that one command filling the gray monotone of the hills with wonderful possibilities of adventure. Her father had made no objection before when she went for a ride. He had merely instructed her to keep to the trails, and if she didn't know the way home, to let the reins lie loose on Yellowjacket's neck and he would bring her to the gate.

Yellowjacket's instinct for direction had not been working that day, however. Lorraine had no sooner left the ranch out of sight behind her than she pretended that she was lost. Yellowjacket had thereupon walked a few rods farther and stopped, patiently indifferent to the location of his oats box. Lorraine had waited until his head began to droop lower and lower, and his switching at flies had become purely automatic. Yellowjacket was going to sleep without making any effort to find the way home. But since Lorraine had not told her father anything about it, his injunction could not have anything to do with the unreliability of the horse.

"Now," she said to the cat, "if three or four bandits would appear on the ridge, over there, and come tearing down into the immediate foreground, jump the gate and surround the house, I'd know this was the real thing. They'd want to make me tell where dad kept his gold or whatever it was they wanted, and they'd have me tied to a chair - and then, cut to Lone Morgan (that's a perfectly *wonderful* name for the lead!) hearing shots and coming on a dead run to the rescue." She picked up the cat and walked slowly down the hard-trodden path to the stable. "But there aren't any bandits, and dad hasn't any gold or anything else worth stealing - Ket, if dad isn't a miser, he's *poor*! And Lone Morgan is merely ashamed of the way I talked to him, and afraid I'll queer myself with the neighbors. No Western lead that *I* ever saw would act like that. Why, he didn't even want to ride home with me, that day.

"And Bob Warfield and his Ford are incidents of the past, and not one soul at the Sawtooth seems to give a darn whether I'm in the country or out of it. Soon as they found out where I belonged, they brought me over here and dropped me and forgot all about me. And that, I suppose, is what they call in fiction the Western spirit!

"Dad looked exactly as if he'd opened the door to a book agent when I came. He - he *tolerates* my presence, Ket! And Frank Johnson's pipe smells to high heaven, and I hate him in the house and 'the boys' - hmhm! The *boys* - Ket, it would be terribly funny, if I didn't have to stay here."

She had reached the corral and stood balancing the cat on a warped top rail, staring disconsolately at Yellowjacket, who stood in a far corner switching at flies and shamelessly displaying all the angularity of his bones under a yellowish hide with roughened hair that was shedding dreadfully, as Lorraine had discovered to her dismay when she removed her green corduroy skirt after riding him. Yellowjacket's lower lip sagged with senility or lack of spirit, Lorraine could not tell which.

"You look like the frontispiece in that horse-doctor book," she remarked, eyeing him with disfavor. "I can't say that comedy hide you've got improves your appearance. You'd be better peeled, I believe."

She heard a chuckle behind her and turned quickly, palm up to shield her eyes from the straight, bright rays of the sun. Now here was a live man, after all, with his hat tilted down over his forehead, a cigarette in one hand and his reins in the other, looking at her and smiling.

"Why don't you peel him, just on a chance?" His smile broadened to a grin, but when Lorraine continued to look at him with a neutral expression in her eyes, he threw away his cigarette and abandoned with it his free-and-easy manner.

"You're Miss Hunter, aren't you? I rode over to see your father. Thought I'd find him somewhere around the corral, maybe."

"You won't, because he's gone for the day. No, I don't know where."

"I - see. Is Mr. Johnson anywhere about?"

"No, I don't believe any one is anywhere about. They were all gone when I got up, a little while ago." Then, remembering that she did not know this man, and that she was a long way from neighbors, she added, "If you'll leave a message I can tell dad when he comes home."

"No-o - I'll ride over to-morrow or next day. I'm the man at Whisper. You can tell him I called, and that I'll call again."

Still he did not go, and Lorraine waited. Some instinct warned her that the man had not yet stated his real reason for coming, and she wondered a little what it could be. He seemed to be watching her covertly, yet she failed to catch any telltale admiration for her in his scrutiny. She decided that his forehead was too narrow to please her, and that his eyes were too close together, and that the lines around his mouth were cruel lines and gave the lie to his smile, which was pleasant enough if you just looked at the smile and paid no attention to anything else in his face.

"You had quite an experience getting out here, they tell me," he observed carelessly; too carelessly, thought Lorraine, who was well schooled in the circumlocutions of delinquent tenants, agents of various sorts and those who crave small gossip of their neighbors. "Heard you were lost up in Rock City all night."

Lorraine looked up at him, startled. "I caught a terrible cold," she said, laughing nervously. "I'm not used to the climate," she added guardedly.

The man fumbled in his pocket and produced smoking material. "Do you mind if I smoke?" he asked perfunctorily.

"Why, no. It doesn't concern me in the slightest degree." Why, she thought confusedly, must she *always* be reminded of that horrible place of rocks? What was it to this man where she had been lost?

"You must of got there about the time the storm broke," the man hazarded after a silence. "It's sure a bad place in a thunderstorm. Them rocks draw lightning. Pretty bad, wasn't it?"

"Lightning is always bad, isn't it?" Lorraine tried to hold her voice steady. "I don't know much about it. We don't have thunderstorms to amount to anything, in Los Angeles. It sometimes does thunder there in the winter, but it is very mild."

With hands that trembled she picked the cat off the rail and started toward the house. "I'll tell dad what you said," she told him, glancing back over her shoulder. When she saw that he had turned his horse and was frankly following her to the house, her heart jumped wildly into her throat, - judging by the feel of it.

"I'm plumb out of matches. I wonder if you can let me have some," he said, still speaking too carelessly to reassure her. "So you stuck it out in Rock City all through that storm! That's more than what I'd want to do."

She did not answer that, but once on the doorstep Lorraine turned and faced him. Quite suddenly it came to her - the knowledge of why she did not like this man. She stared at him, her eyes wide and bright.

"Your hat's brown!" she exclaimed unguardedly. "I - I saw a man with a brown hat -"

He laughed suddenly. "If you stay around here long you'll see a good many," he said, taking off his hat and turning it on his hand before her. "This here hat I traded for yesterday. I had a gray one, but it didn't suit me. Too narrow in the brim. Brown hats are getting to be the style. If I can borrow half a dozen matches, Miss Hunter, I'll be going."

Lorraine looked at him again doubtfully and went after the matches. He thanked her, smiling down at her quizzically. "A man can get along without lots of things, but he's plumb lost without matches. You've maybe saved my life, Miss Hunter, if you only knew it."

She watched him as he rode away, opening the gate and letting himself through without dismounting. He disappeared finally around a small spur of the hill, and Lorraine found her knees trembling under her.

"Ket, you're an awful fool," she exclaimed fiercely. "Why did you let me give myself away to that man? I - I believe he *was* the man.

And if I really did see him, it wasn't my imagination at all. He saw me there, perhaps. Ket, I'm scared! I'm not going to stay on this ranch all alone. I'm going to saddle the family skeleton, and I'm going to ride till dark. There's something queer about that man from Whisper. I'm afraid of him."

After awhile, when she had finished her breakfast and was putting up a lunch, Lorraine picked up the nameless gray cat and holding its head between her slim fingers, looked at it steadily. "Ket, you're the humanest thing I've seen since I left home," she said wistfully. "I *hate* a country where horrible things happen under the surface and the top is just gray and quiet and so dull it makes you want to scream. Lone Morgan lied to me. He lied - he lied!" She hugged the cat impulsively and rubbed her cheek absently against it, so that it began purring immediately.

"Ket - I'm afraid of that man at Whisper!" she breathed miserably against its fur.

## CHAPTER EIGHT

## "IT TAKES NERVE JUST TO HANG ON"

Brit was smoking his pipe after supper and staring at nothing, though his face was turned toward the closed door. Lorraine had washed the dishes and was tidying the room and looking at her father now and then in a troubled, questioning way of which Brit was quite oblivious.

"Dad," she said abruptly, "who is the man at Whisper?"

Brit turned his eyes slowly to her face as if he had not grasped her meaning and was waiting for her to repeat the question. It was evident that his thoughts had pulled away from something that meant a good deal to him.

"Why?"

"A man came this morning, and said he was the man at Whisper, and that he would come again to see you."

Brit took his pipe from his mouth, looked at it and crowded down the tobacco with a forefinger. "He seen me ride away from the ranch, this morning," he said. "He was coming down the Whisper trail as I was taking the fork over to Sugar Spring, Frank and me. What did he say he wanted to see me about?"

"He didn't say. He asked for you and Frank." Lorraine sat down and folded her arms on the oilcloth-covered table. "Dad, what *is* Whisper?"

"Whisper's a camp up against a cliff, over west of here. It belongs to the Sawtooth. Is that all he said? Just that he wanted to see me?"

"He - talked a little," Lorraine admitted, her eyebrows pulled down. "If he saw you leave, I shouldn't think he'd come here and ask for you."

"He knowed I was gone," Brit stated briefly.

With a finger nail Lorraine traced the ugly, brown pattern on the oilcloth. It was not easy to talk to this silent man who was her father, but she had done a great deal of thinking during that long, empty day, and she had reached the point where she was afraid not to speak.

"Dad!"

"What do you want, Raine?"

"Dad, was - has any one around here died, lately?"

"Died? Nobody but Fred Thurman, over here on Granite. He was drug with a horse and killed."

Lorraine caught her breath, saw Brit looking at her curiously and moved closer to him. She wanted to be near somebody just then, and after all, Brit was her father, and his silence was not the inertia of a dull mind, she knew. He seemed bottled-up, somehow, and bitter. She caught his hand and held it, feeling its roughness between her two soft palms.

"Dad, I've got to tell you. I feel trapped, somehow. Did his horse have a white face, dad?"

"Yes, he's a blaze-faced roan. Why?" Brit moved uncomfortably, but he did not take his hand away from her. "What do you know about it, Raine?"

"I saw a man shoot Fred Thurman and push his foot through the stirrup. And, dad, I believe it was that man at Whisper. The one I saw had on a brown hat, and this man wears a brown hat - and I was advised not to tell any one I had been at that place they call Rock City, when the storm came. Dad, would an innocent man - one that didn't have anything to do with a crime - would he try to cover it up afterwards?"

Brit's hand shook when he removed the pipe from his mouth and laid it on the table. His face had turned gray while Lorraine watched him fearfully. He laid his hand on her shoulder, pressing down hard - and at last his eyes met her big, searching ones.

"If he wanted to *live* - in this country - he'd have to. Leastways, he'd have to keep his mouth shut," he said grimly.

"And he'd try to shut the mouths of others -"

"If he cared anything about them, he would. You ain't told anybody what you saw, have yuh?"

Lorraine hid her face against his arm. "Just Lone Morgan, and he thought I was crazy and imagined it. That was in the morning, when he found me. And he - he wanted me to go on thinking it was just a nightmare - that I'd imagined the whole thing. And I did, for awhile. But this man at Whisper tried to find out where I was that night -"

Brit pulled abruptly away from her, got up and opened the door. He stood there for a time, looking out into the gloom of early nightfall. He seemed to be listening, Lorraine thought. When he came back to her his voice was lower, his manner intangibly furtive.

"You didn't tell him anything, did you?" he asked, as if there had been no pause in their talk.

"No - I made him believe I wasn't there. Or I tried to. And dad! As I was going to cross that creek just before you come to Rock City, two men came along on horseback, and I hid before they saw me. They stopped to water their horses, and they were talking. They said something about the TJ had been here a long time, but they would get theirs, and it was like sitting into a poker game with a nickel. They said the little ones aren't big enough to fight the Sawtooth, and they'd carry lead under their hides if they didn't leave. Dad, isn't your brand the TJ? That's what it looks like on Yellowjacket."

Brit did not answer, and when Lorraine was sure that he did not mean to do so, she asked another question. "Dad, why didn't you want me to leave the ranch to-day? I was nervous after that man was here, and I did go."

"I didn't want you riding around the country unless I knew where you went," Brit said. "My brand is the TJ up-and-down. We never call it just the TJ."

"Oh," said Lorraine, relieved. "They weren't talking about you, then. But dad - it's horrible! We simply *can't* let that murder go and not do anything. Because I know that man was shot. I heard the shot fired, and I saw him start to fall off his horse. And the next flash of lightning I saw -"

"Look here, Raine. I don't want you talking about what you saw. I don't want you *thinkin'* about it. What's the use? Thurman's dead and buried. The cor'ner come and held an inquest, and the jury agreed it was an accident. I was on the jury. The sheriff's took charge of his property. You couldn't prove what you saw, even if you was to try." He looked at her very much as Lone Morgan had looked at her. His next words were very nearly what Lone Morgan had said, Lorraine remembered. "You don't know this country like I know it. Folks live in it mainly because they don't go around blatting everything they see and hear and think."

"You have laws, don't you, dad? You spoke about the sheriff -"

The Quirt

"The sheriff!" Brit laughed harshly. "Yes, we got a sheriff, and we got a jail, and a judge - all the makin's of law. But we ain't got one thing that goes with it, and that's justice. You'd best make up your mind like the cor'ner's jury done, that Fred Thurman was drug to death by his horse. That's all that'll ever be proved, and if you can't prove nothing else you better keep your mouth shut."

Lorraine sprang up and stood facing her father, every nerve taut with protest. "You don't mean to tell me, dad, that you and Frank Johnson and Lone Morgan and - everybody in the country are *cowards*, do you?"

Brit looked at her patiently. "No," he said in the tone of acknowledged defeat, "we ain't cowards, Raine. A man ain't a coward when he stands with his hands over his head. Most generally it's because some one's got the drop on 'im."

Lorraine would not accept that. "You think so, because you don't fight," she cried hotly. "No one is holding a gun at your head. Dad! I thought Westerners never quit. It's fight to the finish, always. Why, I've seen one man fight a whole outfit and win. He couldn't be beaten because he wouldn't give up. Why -"

Brit gave her a tolerant glance. "Where'd you see all that, Raine?" He moved to the table picked up his pipe and knocked out the ashes on the stove hearth. His movements were those of an aging man, - yet Brit Hunter was not old, as age is reckoned.

"Well - in stories - but it was reasonable and logical and possible, just the same. If you use your brains you can outwit them, and if you have any nerve -"

Brit made a sound somewhat like a snort. "These days, when politics is played by the big fellows, and the law is used to make money for 'em, it takes nerve just to hang on," he said. "Nobody but a dang fool would fight." Slow anger grew within him. He turned upon Lorraine almost fiercely. "D'yuh think me and Frank could fight the Sawtooth and get anything out of it but a coffin apiece, maybe?" he demanded harshly.

"Don't the Sawtooth *own* this country? Warfield's got the sheriff in his pocket, and the cor'ner, and the judge, and the stock inspector - he's *Senator* Warfield, and what he wants he gets. He gets it through the law that you was talking about a little while ago. What you goin' to do about it? If I had the money and the land and the political pull he's got, mebby I'd have me a sheriff and a judge, too.

"Fred Thurman tried to fight the Sawtooth over a water right he owned and they wanted. They had the case runnin' in court till they like to of took the last dollar he had. He got bull-headed. That water right meant the hull ranch - everything he owned. You can't run a ranch without water. And when he'd took the case up and up till it got to the Supreme Court, and he stood some show of winnin' out - he had an accident. He was drug to death by his horse."

Brit stooped and opened the stove door, seeking a live coal; found none and turned again to Lorraine, shaking his pipe at her for emphasis.

"We try to prove Fred was murdered, and what's the result? Something happens: to me, mebby, or Frank, or both of us. And you can't say, 'Here, I know the Sawtooth had a hand in that.' You got to *prove* it! And when you've proved it," he added bitterly, "you got to have officers that'll carry out the law instead of using it to hog-tie yuh."

His futile, dull anger surged up again. "You call us cowards because we don't git up on our hind legs and fight the Sawtooth. A lot *you* know about courage! You've read stories, and you've saw moving pictures, and you think that's the West - that's the way they do it. One man hold off a hunderd with his gun - and on the other hand, a hunderd men, mebby, ridin' hell-whoopin' after one. You think that's it - that's the way they do it. Hunh!" He lifted the lid of the stove, spat into it as if he were spitting in the face of an enemy, and turned again to Lorraine.

"What you seen - what you say you seen - that was done at night when there wasn't no audience. All the fighting the Sawtooth does is done under cover. *You* won't see none of it - they ain't such fools. And what us small fellers do, we do it quiet, too. We ain't ridin' up and down the trail, flourishin' our six-shooters and yellin' to the Sawtooth to come on and we'll clean 'em up!"

"But you're fighting just the same, aren't you, dad? You're not letting them -"

"We're makin' out to live here - and we've been doin' it for twenty-five year," Brit told her, with a certain grim dignity. "We've still got a few head uh stock left - enough to live on. Playin' poker with a nickel, mebby - but we manage to ante, every hand so fur." His mind returned to the grisly thing Lorraine had seen.

"We can't run down the man that got Fred Thurman, supposin' he was killed, as you say. That's what the law is paid to do. If Lone Morgan told you not to talk about it, he told you right. He was talking for your own good. What about Al - the man from Whisper? You didn't tell *him*, did you?"

His tone, the suppressed violence of his manner, frightened Lorraine. She moved farther away from him.

"I didn't tell him anything. He was curious but - I only said I knew him because he was wearing a brown hat, and the man that shot Mr. Thurman had a brown hat. I didn't say all that. I just mentioned the hat. And he said there were lots of brown hats in the country. He said he had traded for that one, just yesterday. He said his own hat was gray."

Brit stared at her, his jaw sagging a little, his eyes growing vacant with the thoughts he hid deep in his mind. He slumped down into his chair and leaned forward, his arms resting on his knees, his fingers clasped loosely. After a little he tilted his head and looked up at her.

"You better go to bed," he told her stolidly. "And if you're going to live at the Quirt, Raine, you'll have to learn to keep your mouth shut. I ain't blaming you - but you told too much to Al Woodruff. Don't talk to him no more, if he comes here when I'm gone." He put out a hand, beckoning her to him, sorry for his harshness. Lorraine went to him and knelt beside him, slipping an arm around his neck while she hid her face on his shoulder.

"I won't be a nuisance, dad - really, I won't," she said. "I - I can shoot a gun. I never shot one with bullets in, but I could. And I learned to do lots of things when I was working in that play West I thought was real. It isn't like I thought. There's no picture stuff in the real West, I guess; they don't do things that way. But - what I want you to know is that if they're fighting you they'll have to fight me, too.

"I don't mean movie stuff, honestly I don't. I'm in this thing now, and you'll have to count me, same as you count Jim and Sorry. Won't you please feel that I'm one more in the game, dad, and not just another responsibility? I'll herd cattle, or do whatever there is to do. And I'll keep my mouth shut, too. I can't stay here, day after day, doing nothing but sweep and dust two rooms and fry potatoes and bacon for you at night. Dad, I'll go *crazy* if you don't let me into your life!

"Dad, if you knew the stunts I've done in the last three years! It was make-believe West, but I learned things just the same." She kissed him on the unshaven cheek nearest her, - and thought of the kisses she had breathed upon the cheeks of story fathers with due care for the make-up on her lips. Just because this was real, she kissed him again with the frank vigor of a child.

"Dad," she said wheedlingly, "I think you might scare up something that I can really ride. Yellowjacket is safe, but - but you have real *live* horses on the ranch, haven't you? You must *not* go judging me by the palms and the bay windows of the Casa Grande. That's where I've slept, the last few years when I wasn't off on location - but it's just as sensible to think I don't know anything else, as it would be for me to think you can't do anything but skim milk and fry bacon and make sour-dough bread, just because I've seen you do it!"

Brit laughed and patted her awkwardly on the back. "If you was a boy, I'd set you up as a lawyer," he said with an attempt at playfulness. "I kinda thought you could ride. I seen how you piled onto old Yellowjacket and the way you held your reins. It runs in the blood, I guess. I'll see what I can do in the way of a horse. Ole Yellowjacket used to be a real rim-rider, but he's gitting old; gitting old - same as me."

"You're not! You're just letting yourself *feel* old. And am I one of the outfit, dad?"

"I guess so - only there ain't going to be any of this hell-whoopin' stuff, Raine. You can't travel these trails at a long lope with yore hair flyin' out behind and - and all that damn foolishness. I've saw 'em in the movin' pitchers -"

Lorraine blushed, and was thankful that her dad had not watched her work in that serial. For that matter, she hoped that Lone Morgan would never stray into a movie where any of her pictures were being shown.

"I'm serious, dad. I don't want to make a show of myself. But if you'll feel that I can be a help instead of a handicap, that's what I want. And if it comes to fighting -"

Brit pushed her from him impatiently. "There yuh go - fight - fight - and I told yuh there ain't any fighting going on. Nothing more'n a fight to hang on and make a living. That means straight, hard work and mindin' your own business. If you want to help at that -"

"I do," said Raine quietly, getting to her feet. Her legacy of stubbornness set her lips firmly together. "That's exactly what I mean. Good night, dad."

Brit answered her noncommittally, apparently sunk already in his own musings. But his lips drew in to suppress a smile when he saw, from the corner of his eyes, that Lorraine was winding the alarm on the cheap kitchen clock, and that she set the hand carefully and took the clock with her to bed.

## CHAPTER NINE

## THE EVIL EYE OF THE SAWTOOTH

Oppression is a growth that flourishes best in the soil of opportunity. It seldom springs into full power at once. The Sawtooth Cattle Company had begun much as its neighbors had begun: with a tract of land, cattle, and the ambition for prospering. Senator Warfield had then been plain Bill Warfield, manager of the outfit, who rode with his men and saw how his herds increased, - saw too how they might increase faster under certain conditions. At the outset he was not, perhaps, more unscrupulous than some of his neighbors. True, if a homesteader left his claim for a longer time than the law allowed him, Bill Warfield would choose one of his own men to file a contest on that claim. The man's wages would be paid. Witnesses were never lacking to swear to the improvements he had made, and after the patent had been granted the homesteader (for the contestant always won, in that country) the Sawtooth, would pay him for the land. Frequently a Sawtooth man would file upon land before any other man had claimed it. Sometimes a Sawtooth man would purchase a relinquishment from some poor devil of a claim-holder who seemed always to have bad luck, and so became discouraged and ready to sell. An intelligent man like Bill Warfield could acquire much land in this manner, give him time enough.

In much the same manner his herds increased. He bought out small ranchers who were crowded to the selling point in one way or another. They would find themselves fenced off from water, the Sawtooth having acquired the water rights to creek or spring.

Or they would be hemmed in with fenced fields and would find it next to impossible to make use of the law which gave them the right to "condemn" a road through. They would not be openly assailed, - Bill Warfield was an intelligent man. A dozen brands were recorded in the name of the Sawtooth Cattle Company, and if a small rancher found his calf crop shorter than it should be, he might think as he pleased, but he would have no tangible proof that his calves wore a Sawtooth brand.

Inevitably it became necessary now and then to stop a mouth that was ready to speak unwelcome truths. But if a Sawtooth man were known to have committed violence, the Sawtooth itself was the first to put the sheriff on his trail. If the man successfully dodged the sheriff and made his way to parts unknown, the Sawtooth could shrug its shoulders and wash its hands of him.

Then whispers were heard that the Sawtooth had on its pay roll men who were paid to kill and to leave no trace. So many heedless ones crossed the Sawtooth's path to riches! Fred Thurman had been one; a "bull-headed cuss" who had the temerity to fight back when the Sawtooth calmly laid claim to the first water rights to Granite Creek, having bought it, they said, with the placer claim of an old miner who had prospected along the headwaters of Granite at the base of Bear Top.

By that time the Sawtooth had grown to a power no poor man could hope to defeat. Bill Warfield was Senator Warfield, and Senator Warfield was a power in the political world that immediately surrounded him. Since his neighboring ranchmen had not been able to prevent his steady climbing to the position he now held, they had small hope of pulling him down. Brit was right. They did well to hang on and continue living in that country.

An open killing, one that would attract the attention of the outside world, might be avenged. The man who committed the crime might be punished, - if public opinion were sufficiently massed against him. In that case Senator Warfield would cry loudest for justice. But it would take a stronger man than the country held to raise the question of Fred Thurman's death and take even the first steps toward proving it a murder.

"It ain't that they can *do* anything, Mr. Warfield," the man from Whisper said guardedly, urging his horse close to the machine that stood in the trail from Echo. It was broad day - a sun-scorched day to boot - and Senator Warfield perspired behind the wheel of his car. "It's the talk they may get started."

"What have they said? The girl was at the ranch for several days. She didn't talk there, or Hawkins would have told me."

"She was sick. I saw her the other day at the Quirt, and she more'n half recognized me. Hell! How'd *I* know she was in there among them rocks? Everybody that was apt to be riding through was accounted for, and I knew there wasn't any one coming horseback or with a rig. My hearing's pretty good."

Warfield moved the spark lever up and down on the wheel while he thought. "Well," he said carefully at last, "if you're falling down in your work, what are you whining about it to me for? What do you want?"

Al moistened his lips with his tongue. "I want to know how far I can go. It's been hands off the Quirt, up to now. And the Quirt's beginning to think it can get away with most anything. They've throwed a fence across the pass through from Sugar Spring to Whisper. That sends us away around by Three Creek. You can't trail stock across Granite Ridge, nor them lava ledges. If it's going to be hands off, I want to know it. There's other places I'd rather live in, if the Quirt's going to raise talk about Fred Thurman."

Senator Warfield pulled at his collar and tie as if they choked him. "The Quirt has made no trouble," he said. "Of course, if they begin throwing fences across our stock trails and peddling gossip, that is another story. I expect you to protect our interests, of course. And I have never made a practice of dictating to you. In this case" - he sent a sharp glance at Al - "it seems to me your interests are involved more than ours. As to Fred Thurman, I don't know anything about it. I was not here when he died, and I have never seen this girl of Brit's who seems to worry you. She doesn't interest me, one way or the other."

"She seems to interest Bob a whole lot," Al said maliciously. "He rode over to see her yesterday. She wasn't home, though."

Senator Warfield seemed unmoved by this bit of news, wherefore Al returned to the main issue.

"Do I get a free hand, or don't I?" he insisted. "They can't be let peddle talk - not if I stay around here."

Senator Warfield considered the matter.

"The girl's got the only line on me," Al went on. "The inquest was as clean as I ever saw. Everything all straight - and then, here she comes up -"

"If you know how to stop a woman's mouth, Al, you can make a million a month telling other men." Senator Warfield smiled at him. Then he leaned across the front seat and added impressively, "Bear one thing in mind, Al. The Sawtooth cannot permit itself to become involved in any scandal, nor in any killing cases. We're just at the most crucial point with our reclamation project, over here on the flat. The legislature is willing to make an appropriation for the building of the canal, and in two or three months at the latest we should begin selling agricultural tracts to the public. The State will also throw open the land it had withdrawn from settlement, pending the floating of this canal project. More than ever the integrity of the Sawtooth Cattle Company must be preserved, since it has come out openly as a backer of the irrigation company. Nothing - *nothing* must be permitted to stand in the way."

He removed his thin driving cap and wiped his perspiring forehead. "I'm sorry this all happened - as it has turned out," he said, with real regret in his tone. "But since it did happen, I must rely upon you to - to - er -"

"I guess I understand," Al grinned sardonically. "I just wanted you to know how things is building up. The Quirt's kinda overreached itself. I didn't want you comin' back on me for trying to keep their feet outa the trough. I want you to know things is pretty damn ticklish right now, and it's going to take careful steppin'."

"Well, don't let your foot slip, Al," Senator Warfield warned him. "The Sawtooth would hate to lose you; you're a good man."

"Oh, I get yuh," Al retorted. "My foot ain't going to slip - If it did, the Sawtooth would be the first to pile onto my back!" The last sentence was not meant for the senator's ears. Al had backed his horse, and Senator Warfield was stepping on the starter. But it would not have mattered greatly if he had heard, for this was a point quite thoroughly understood by them both.

The Warfield car went on, lurching over the inequalities of the narrow road. Al shook his horse into a shambling trot, picking his way carelessly through the scattered sage.

His horse traveled easily, now and then lifting a foot high to avoid rock or exposed root, or swerving sharply around obstacles too high to step over. Al very seldom traveled along the beaten trails, though there was nothing to deter him now save an inherent tendency toward secretiveness of his motives, destinations and whereabouts. If the country was open, you would see Al Woodruff riding at some distance from the trail - or you would not see him at all, if there were gullies in which he could conceal himself. He was always "line-riding," or hunting stray stock - horses, usually - or striking across to some line-camp of the Sawtooth, on business which he was perfectly willing to state.

But you will long ago have guessed that he was the evil eye of the Sawtooth Company. He took no orders save such general ones as Senator Warfield had just given him. He gave none. Whatever he did he did alone, and he took no man into his confidence. It is more than probable that Senator Warfield would never have known to a certainty that Al was responsible for Thurman's death, if Al had not been worried over the Quirt's possible knowledge of the crime and anxious to know just how far his power might go.

Ostensibly he was in charge of the camp at Whisper, a place far enough off the beaten trails to free him from chance visitors. The Sawtooth kept many such camps occupied by men whose duty it was to look after the Sawtooth cattle that grazed near; to see that stock did not "bog down" in the tricky sand of the adjacent water holes and die before help came, and to fend off any encroachments of the smaller cattle owners, - though these were growing fewer year by year, thanks to the weeding-out policy of the Sawtooth and the cunning activities of such as Al Woodruff.

It may sound strange to say that the Sawtooth country had not had a real "killing" for years, though accidental deaths had been rather frequent. One man, for instance, had fallen over a ledge and broken his neck, presumably while drunk. Another had bought a few sticks of dynamite to open up a spring on his ranch, and at the inquest which followed the jury had returned a verdict of "death caused by being blown up by the accidental discharge of dynamite." A sheepman was struck by lightning, according to the coroner, and his widow had been glad to sell ranch and sheep very cheaply to the Sawtooth and return to her relatives in Montana. The Sawtooth had shipped the sheep within a month and turned the ranch into another line-camp.

You will see that Senator Warfield had every reason to be sincere when he called Al Woodruff a good man; good for the Sawtooth interests, that means. You will also see that Brit Hunter had reasons for believing that the business of ranching in the Sawtooth country might be classed as extra hazardous, and for saying that it took nerve just to hang on.

That is why Al rode oblivious to his surroundings, meditating no doubt upon the best means of preserving the "integrity" of the Sawtooth and at the same time soothing effectively the ticklishness of the situation of which he had complained. It was his business to find the best means. It was for just such work that the Sawtooth paid him - secretly, to be sure - better wages than the foreman, Hawkins, received. Al was conscientious and did his best to earn his wages; not because he particularly loved killing and spying as a sport, but because the Sawtooth had bought his loyalty for a price, and so long as he felt that he was getting a square deal from them, he would turn his hand against any man that stood in their way. He was a Sawtooth man, and he fought the enemies of the Sawtooth as matter-of-factly as a soldier will fight for his country. To his unimaginative mind there was sufficient justification in that attitude. As for the ease with which he planned to kill and cover his killing under the semblance of accident, he would have said, if you could make him speak of it, that he was not squeamish. They'd all have to die some day, anyway.

## CHAPTER TEN

## ANOTHER SAWTOOTH "ACCIDENT"

Frank Johnson rose from the breakfast table, shaved a splinter off the edge of the water bench for a toothpick and sharpened it carefully while he looked at Brit.

"You goin' after them posts, or shall I?" he inquired glumly, which, by the way, was his normal tone. "Jim and Sorry oughta git the post holes all dug to-day. One of us better take a look through that young stock in the lower field, too, and see if there's any more sign uh blackleg. Which you ruther do?"

Brit tilted his chair backward so that he could reach the coffeepot on the stove hearth. "I'll haul down the posts," he decided carelessly. "They're easy loaded, and I guess my back's as good as yourn."

"All you got to do is skid 'em down off'n the bank onto the wagon," Frank said. "I wisht you'd go on up where we cut them last ones and git my sweater, Brit. I musta left it hanging on a bush right close to where I was workin'."

Brit's grunt signified assent, and Frank went out. Jim and Sorry, the two unpicturesque cowboys of whom Lorraine had complained to the cat had already departed with pick and shovel to their unromantic task of digging post holes. Each carried a most unattractive lunch tied in a flour sack behind the cantle of his saddle. Lorraine had done her conscientious best, but with lumpy, sour-dough bread, cold bacon and currant jelly of that kind which is packed in wooden kegs, one can't do much with a cold lunch. Lorraine wondered how much worse it would look after it had been tied on the saddle for half a day; wondered too what those two silent ones got out of life, - what they looked forward to, what was their final goal. For that matter she frequently wondered what there was in life for any of them, shut into that deadly monotony of sagebrush and rocks interspersed with little, grassy meadows where the cattle fed listlessly.

Even the sinister undercurrent of antagonism against the Quirt could not whip her emotions feeling that she was doing anything more than live the restricted, sordid little life of a poorly equipped ranch. She had ridden once with Frank Johnson to look through a bunch of cattle, but it had been nothing more than a hot, thirsty, dull ride, with a wind that blew her hat off in spite of pins and tied veil, and with a companion who spoke only when he was spoken to and then as briefly as possible.

Her father would not talk again as he had talked that night. She had tried to make him tell her more about the Sawtooth and had gotten nothing out of him. The man from Whisper, whom Brit had spoken of as Al, had not returned. Nor had the promised saddle horse materialized. The boys were too busy to run in any horses, her father had told her shortly when she reminded him of his promise. When the fence was done, maybe he could rustle her another horse, - and then he had added that he didn't see what ailed Yellowjacket, for all the riding she was likely to do.

"Straight hard work and minding your own business," her father had said, and it seemed to Lorraine after three or four days of it that he had summed up the life of a cattleman's daughter in a masterly manner which ought to be recorded among Famous Sayings like "War is hell" and "Don't give up the ship."

On this particular morning Lorraine's spirits were at their lowest ebb. If it were not for the new stepfather, she would return to the Casa Grande, she told herself disgustedly. And if it were not for the belief among all her acquaintances that she was queening it over the cattle-king's vast domain, she would return and find work again in motion pictures. But she could not bring herself to the point of facing the curiosity and the petty gossip of the studios. She would be expected to explain satisfactorily why she had left the real West for the mimic West of Hollywood. She did not acknowledge to herself that she also could not face the admission of failure to carry out what she had begun.

She had told her dad that she wanted to fight with him, even though "fighting" in this case meant washing the coarse clothing of her father and Frank, scrubbing the rough, warped boards of the cabin floor, and frying ranch-cured bacon for every meal, and in making butter to sell, and counting the eggs every night and being careful to use only the cracked ones for cooking.

She hated every detail of this crude housekeeping, from the chipped enamel dishpan to the broom that was all one-sided, and the pillow slips which were nothing more nor less than sugar sacks. She hated it even more than she had hated the Casa Grande and her mother's frowsy mentality. But because she could see that she made life a little more comfortable for her dad, because she felt that he needed her, she would stay and assure herself over and over that she was staying merely because she was too proud to go back to the old life and own the West a failure.

She was sweeping the doorstep with the one-sided broom when Brit drove out through the gate and up the trail which she knew led eventually to Sugar Spring. The horses, sleek in their new hair and skittish with the change from hay to new grass, danced over the rough ground so that the running gear of the wagon, with its looped log-chain, which would later do duty as a brake on the long grade down from timber line on the side of Spirit Canyon, rattled and banged over the rocks with a clatter that could be heard for half a mile. Lorraine looked after her father enviously. If she were a boy she would be riding on that sack of hay tied to the "hounds" for a seat. But, being a girl, it had never occurred to Brit that she might like to go, - might even be useful to him on the trip.

"I suppose if I told dad I could drive that team as well as he can, he'd just look at me and think I was crazy," she thought resentfully and gave the broom a spiteful fling toward a presumptuous hen that had approached too closely. "If I'd asked him to let me go along he'd have made some excuse - oh, I'm beginning to know dad! He thinks a woman's place is in the house - preferably the kitchen. And here I've thought all my life that cowgirls did nothing but ride around and warn people about stage holdups and everything! I'd just like to know how a girl would ever have a chance to know what was going on in the country, unless she heard the men talking while she poured their coffee. Only this bunch don't talk at all. They just gobble and go."

She went in then and shut the door with a slam. Up on the ridge Al Woodruff lowered his small binocular and eased away from the spot where he had been crouching behind a bush. Every one on the Quirt ranch was accounted for. As well as if he had sat at their breakfast table Al knew where each man's work would take him that day. As for the girl, she was safe at the ranch for the day, probably. If she did take a ride later on, it would probably be up the ridge between the Quirt and Thurman's ranch, and sit for an hour or so just looking. That ride was beginning to be a habit of hers, Al had observed, so that he considered her accounted for also.

He made his way along the side hill to where his horse was tied to a bush, mounted and rode away with his mind pretty much at ease. Much more at ease than it would have been had he read what was in Lorraine's mind when, she slammed that door.

Up above Sugar Spring was timber. By applying to the nearest Forest Supervisor a certain amount could be had for ranch improvements upon paying a small sum for the "stumpage." The Quirt had permission to cut posts for their new fence which Al Woodruff had reported to his boss.

As he drove up the trail, which was in places barely passable for a wagon, Brit was thinking of that fence. The Sawtooth would object to it, he knew, since it cut off one of their stock trails and sent them around through rougher country. Just what form their objection would take, Brit did not know. Deep in his intrepid soul he hoped that the Sawtooth would at last show its hand openly. He had liked Fred Thurman, and what Lorraine had told him went much deeper than she knew. He wanted to bring them into the open where he could fight with some show of winning.

"I'll git Bill Warfield yet - and git him right," was the gist of his musings. "He's bound to show his head, give him time enough. Him and his killers can't always keep under cover. Let 'em come at me about that fence! It's on my land - the Quirt's got a right to fence every foot of land that belongs to 'em."

All the way over the ridge and across the flat and up the steep, narrow road along the edge of Spirit Canyon, Brit dwelt upon the probable moves of the Sawtooth. They would wait, he thought, until the fence was completed and they had made a trail around through the lava rocks. They would not risk any move at present; they would wait and tacitly accept the fence, or pretend to accept it, as a natural inconvenience. But Brit did not deceive himself that they would remain passive. That it had been "hands off the Quirt" he did not know, but attributed the Quirt's immunity to careful habits and the fact that they had never come to the point where their interests actually clashed with the Sawtooth.

It never occurred to him therefore that he was slated for an accident that day if the details could be conveniently arranged.

It was a long trail to Sugar Spring, and from there up Spirit Canyon the climb was so tedious and steep that Brit took a full hour for the trip, resting the team often because they were soft from the new grass diet and sweated easily. They lost none of their spirit, however, and when the road was steepest nagged at each other with head-shakings and bared teeth, and ducked against each other in pretended fright at every unusual rock or bush.

At the top he was forced to drive a full half mile beyond the piled posts to a flat large enough to turn around. All this took time, especially since Caroline, the brown mare, would rather travel ten miles straight ahead than go backward ten feet. Brit was obliged to "take it out of her" with the rein ends and his full repertoire of opprobrious epithets before he could cramp the wagon and head them down the trail again.

At the post pile he unhitched the team for safety's sake and tied them to trees, where he fed them a little grain in nose bags. He was absorbed now in his work and thought no more about the Sawtooth. He fastened the log chain to the rear wheels to brake the wagon on the long grade down the canyon, loaded the wagon with posts, bound them fast with a lighter chain he had brought for the purpose, ate his own lunch and decided that, since he had made fair time and would arrive home too early to do the chores and too late to start any other job, he would cruise farther up the mountain side and see what was the prospect of getting out logs enough for an addition to the cabin.

Now that Raine was going to live with him, two rooms were not enough. Brit wanted to make her as happy as he could, in his limited fashion. He had for some days been planning a "settin' room and bedroom" for her. She would be having beaux after awhile when she got acquainted, he supposed. He could not deny her the privilege; she was young and she was, in Brit's opinion, the best looking girl he had ever seen, not even excepting Minnie, her mother. But he hoped she wouldn't go off and get married the first thing she did, - and one good way to prevent that, he reasoned, was to make her comfortable with him. He had noticed how pleased she was that their cabin was of logs. She had even remarked that she could not understand how a rancher would ever want to build a board shack if there was any timber to be had. Well, timber was to be had, and she should have her log house, though the hauling was not going to be any sunshine, in Brit's opinion. With his axe he walked through the timber, craning upward for straight tree trunks and lightly blazing the ones he would want, the occasional axe strokes sounding distinctly in the quiet air.

Lorraine heard them as she rode old Yellowjacket puffing up the grade, following the wagon marks, and knew that she was nearing the end of her journey, - for which Yellowjacket, she supposed, would be thankful. She had started not more than an hour later than her father, but the team had trotted along more briskly than her poor old nag would travel, so that she did not overtake her dad as she had hoped.

She was topping the last climb when she saw the team tied to the trees, and at the same moment she caught a glimpse of a man who crawled out from under the load of posts and climbed the slope farther on. She was on the point of calling out to him, thinking that he was her dad, when he disappeared into the brush. At the same moment she heard the stroke of an axe over to the right of where the man was climbing.

She was riding past the team when Caroline humped her back and kicked viciously at Yellowjacket, who plunged straight down off the trail without waiting to see whether Caroline's aim was exact. He slid into a juniper thicket and sat down looking very perplexed and very permanently placed there. Lorraine stepped off on the uphill side of him, thanked her lucky stars she had not broken a leg, and tried to reassure Yellowjacket and to persuade him that no real harm had been done him. Straightway she discovered that Yellowjacket had a mind of his own and that a pessimistic mind. He refused to scramble back into the trail, preferring to sit where he was, or since Lorraine made that too uncomfortable, to stand where he had been sitting. Yellowjacket, I may explain, owned a Roman nose, a pendulous lower lip and drooping eyelids. Those who know horses will understand.

By the time Lorraine had bullied and cajoled him into making a somewhat circuitous route to the road, where he finally appeared some distance above the point of his descent, Brit was there, hitching the team to the wagon.

"What yuh doing up there?" he wanted to know, looking up with some astonishment.

Lorraine furnished him with details and her opinion of both Caroline and Yellow jacket. "I simply refuse to ride this comedy animal another mile," she declared with some heat. "I'll drive the team and you can ride him home, or he can be tied on behind the wagon."

"He won't lead," Brit objected. "Yeller's all right if you make up your mind to a few failin's. You go ahead and ride him home. You sure can't drive this team."

"I can!" Lorraine contended. "I've driven four horses - I guess I can drive two, all right."

"Well, you ain't going to," Brit stated with a flat finality that abruptly ended the argument.

Lorraine had never before been really angry with her father. She struck Yellowjacket with her quirt and sent him sidling past the wagon and the tricky Caroline, too stubborn to answer her dad when he called after her that she had better ride behind the load. She went on, making Yellowjacket trot when he did not want to trot down hill.

Behind her she heard the chuck-chuck of the loaded wagon. Far ahead she heard some one whistling a high, sweet melody which had the queer, minor strains of some old folk song. For just a few bars she heard it, and then it was stilled, and the road dipping steeply before her seemed very lonely, its emptiness cooling her brief anger to a depression that had held her too often in its grip since that terrible night of the storm. For the first time she looked back at her father lurching along on the load and at the team looking so funny with the collars pushed up on their necks with the weight of the load behind.

With a quick impulse of penitence she waved her hand to Brit, who waved back at her. Then she went on, feeling a bit less alone in the world. After all, he was her dad, and his life had been hard. If he failed to understand her and her mental hunger for real companionship, perhaps she also failed to understand him.

They had left the timber line now and had come to the lip of the canyon itself. Lorraine looked down its steep, rock-roughened sides and thought how her old director would have raved over its possibilities in the way of "stunts." Yellow jacket, she noticed, kept circumspectly to the center of the trail and eyed the canyon with frank disfavor.

She did not know at just what moment she became aware of trouble behind her. It may have been Yellowjacket, turning his head sidewise and abruptly quickening his pace that warned her. It may have been the difference in the sound of the wagon and the impact of the horses' hoofs on the rocky trail. She turned and saw that something had gone wrong. They were coming down upon her at a sharp trot, stepping high, the wagon tongue thrust up between their heads as they tried to hold back the load.

Brit yelled to her then to get out of the way, and his voice was harsh and insistent. Lorraine looked at the steep bank to the right, knew instinctively that Yellowjacket would never have time to climb it before the team was upon them, and urged him to a lope. She glanced back again, saw that the team was not running away, that they were trying to hold the wagon, and that it was gaining momentum in spite of them.

"Jump, dad!" she called and got no answer. Brit was sitting braced with his feet far apart, holding and guiding the team. "He won't jump - he wouldn't jump - any more than I would," she chattered to herself, sick with fear for him, while she lashed her own horse to keep out of their way.

The next she knew, the team was running, their eyeballs staring, their front feet flung high as they lunged panic-stricken down the trail. The load was rocking along behind them. Brit was still braced and clinging to the reins.

Panic seized Yellowjacket. He, too, went lunging down that trail, his head thrown from side to side that he might watch the thing that menaced him, heedless of the fact that danger might lie ahead of him also. Lorraine knew that he was running senselessly, that he might leave the trail at any bend and go rolling into the canyon.

A sense of unreality seized her. It could not be deadly earnest, she thought. It was so exactly like some movie thrill, planned carefully in advance, rehearsed perhaps under the critical eye of the director, and done now with the camera man turning calmly the little crank and counting the number of film feet the scene would take. A little farther and she would be out of the scene, and men stationed ahead would ride up and stop her horse for her and tell her how well she had "put it over."

She looked over her shoulder and saw them still coming. It was real. It was terribly real, the way that team was fleeing down the grade. She had never seen anything like that before, never seen horses so frantically trying to run from the swaying load behind them. Always, she had been accustomed to moderation in the pace and a slowed camera to speed up the action on the screen. Yellowjacket, too - she had never ridden at that terrific speed down hill. Twice she lost a stirrup and grabbed the saddle horn to save herself from going over his head.

They neared a sharp turn, and it took all her strength to pull her horse to the inside and save him from plunging off down the canyon's side. The nose of the hill hid for a moment her dad, and in that moment she heard a crash and knew what had happened. But she could not stop; Yellowjacket had his ears laid back flat on his senseless head, and the bit clamped tight in his teeth.

She heard the crash repeated in diminuendo farther down in the canyon. There was no longer the rattle of the wagon coming down the trail, the sharp staccato of pounding hoofs.

## CHAPTER ELEVEN

## SWAN TALKS WITH HIS THOUGHTS

Lorraine, following instinct rather than thought, pulled Yellowjacket into the first opening that presented itself. This was a narrow, rather precipitous gully that seamed the slope just beyond the bend. The bushes there whipped her head and shoulders cruelly as the horse forged in among them, but they trapped him effectually where the gully narrowed to a point. He stopped perforce, and Lorraine was out of the saddle and running down to the trail before she quite realized what she was doing.

At the bend she looked down, saw the marks where the wagon had gone over, scraping rocks and bushes from its path. Fence posts were strewn at all angles down the incline, and far down a horse was standing with part of the harness on him and with his head drooping dispiritedly. Her father she could not see, nor the other horse, nor the wagon. A clump of young trees hid the lower declivity. Lorraine did not stop to think of what she would find down there. Sliding, running, she followed the traces of the wreck to where the horse was standing. It was Caroline, looking very dejected but apparently unhurt, save for skinned patches here and there where she had rolled over rocks.

A little farther, just beyond the point of the grove which they seemed to have missed altogether, lay the other horse and what was left of the wagon. Brit she did not see at all. She searched the bushes, looked under the wagon, and called and called.

A full-voiced shout answered her from farther up the canyon, and she ran stumbling toward the sound, too agonized to shed tears or to think very clearly. It was not her father's voice; she knew that beyond all doubt. It was no voice that she had ever heard before. It had a clear resonance that once heard would not have been easily forgotten. When she saw them finally, her father was being propped up in a half-sitting position, and the strange man was holding something to his lips.

"Just a little water. I carry me a bottle of water always in my pocket," said Swan, glancing up at her when she had reached them. "It sometimes makes a man's head think better when he has been hurt, if he can drink a little water or something."

Brit swallowed and turned his face away from the tilted bottle. "I jumped - but I didn't jump quick enough," he muttered thickly. "The chain pulled loose. Where's the horses, Raine?"

"They're all right. Caroline's standing over there. Are you hurt much, dad?" It was a futile question, because Brit was already going off into unconsciousness.

"He's hurt pretty bad," Swan declared honestly, looking up at her with his eyes grown serious. "I was across the walley and I saw him coming down the road like rolling rocks down a hill. I came quick. Now we make stretcher, I think, and carry him home. I could take him on my back, but that is hurting him too much." He looked at her - through her, it seemed to Lorraine. In spite of her fear, in spite of her grief, she felt that Swan was reading her very soul, and she backed away from him.

"I could help your father very much," he said soberly, "but I should tell you a secret if I do that. I should maybe ask that you tell a lie if somebody asks questions. Could you do that, Miss?"

"Lie?" Lorraine laughed uncertainly. "I'd *kill!* - if that would help dad."

Swan was folding his coat very carefully and placing it under Brit's head. "My mother I love like that," he said, without looking up. "My mother I love so well that I talk with my thoughts to her sometimes. You believe people can talk with their thoughts?"

"I don't know - what's that got to do with helping dad?" Lorraine knelt beside Brit and began stroking his forehead softly, as is the soothing way of women with their sick.

"I could send my thought to my mother. I could say to her that a man is hurt and that a doctor must come very quickly to the Quirt ranch. I could do that, Miss, but I should not like it if people knew that I did it. They would maybe say that I am crazy. They would laugh at me, and it is not right to laugh at those things."

"I'm not laughing. If you can do it, for heaven's sake go ahead! I don't believe it, but I won't tell any one, if that's what you want."

"If some neighbors should ask, 'How did that doctor come so quick?' -"

"I'd rather lie and say I sent for him, than say that you or any one else sent a telepathic message. That would sound more like a lie than a lie would. How are we going to make a stretcher? We've got to get him home, somehow -"

"At my cabin is blankets," Swan told her briskly. "I can climb the hill - it is up there. In a little while I will come back."

He started off without waiting to see what Lorraine would have to say about it, and with some misgivings she watched him run down to the canyon's bottom and go forging up the opposite side with a most amazing speed and certainty. In travel pictures she had seen mountain sheep climb like that, and she likened him now to one of them. It seemed a shame that he was a bit crazy, she thought; and immediately she recalled his perfect assurance when he told her of sending thought messages to his mother. She had heard of such things, she had even read a little on the subject, but it had never seemed to her a practical means of communicating.

Calling a doctor, for instance, seemed to Lorraine rather far-fetched an application of what was at best but a debatable theory.

Considering the distance, he was back in a surprisingly short time with two blankets, a couple of light poles and a flask of brandy. He seemed as fresh and unwinded as if he had gone no farther than the grove, and he wore, more than ever, his air of cheerful assurance.

"The doctor will be there," he remarked, just as if it were the simplest thing in the world. "We can carry him to Fred Thurman's. There I can get horses and a wagon, and you will not have to carry so far. And when we get to your ranch the doctor will be there, I think. He is starting now. We will hurry. I will fix it so you need not carry much. It is just to make it steady for me."

While he talked he was working on the stretcher. He had a rope, and he was knotting it in a long loop to the poles. Lorraine wondered why, until he had lifted her father and placed him on the stretcher and placed the loop over his own head and under one arm, as a ploughman holds the reins, so that his hands may be free.

"If you will carry the front," said Swan politely, "it will not be heavy for you like this. But you will help me keep it steady."

Lorraine was past discussing anything. She obeyed him silently, lifting the end of the stretcher and leading the way down to the canyon's bottom, where Swan assured her they could walk quite easily and would save many detours which the road above must take. At the bottom Swan stopped her so that he might shorten the rope and take more of the weight on his shoulders. She protested half-heartedly, but Swan only laughed.

"I am strong like a mule," he said. "You should see me wrestle with somebody. Clear over my head - I can carry a man in my hands. This is so you can walk fast. Three miles straight down we come to Thurman's ranch, where I get the horses. It's funny how hills make a road far around. Just three miles - that's all. I have walked many times."

Lorraine did not answer him. She felt that he was talking merely to keep her from worrying, and she was fairly sick with anxiety and did not hear half of what he was saying. She was nervously careful about choosing her steps so that she would not stumble and jolt her father. She did not believe that he was wholly unconscious, for she had seen his eyelids tighten and his lips twitch several times, when she was waiting for Swan. He had seemed to be in pain and to be trying to hide the fact from her. She felt that Swan knew it, else he would have talked of her dad, would at least have tried to reassure her. But it is difficult to speak of a person who hears what you are saying, and Swan was talking of everything, it seemed to her, except the man they were carrying.

She wondered if it were really true that Swan had sent a call through space for a doctor; straightway she would call herself crazy for even considering for a moment its possibility. If he could do that - but of course he couldn't. He must just imagine it.

Many times Swan had her lower the stretcher to the ground, and would make a great show of rubbing his arms and easing his shoulder muscles. Whenever Lorraine looked full into his face he would grin at her as though nothing was wrong, and when they came to a clear-running stream he emptied the water bottle, dipped up a little fresh water, added brandy, and lifted Brit's head very gently and gave him a drink. Brit opened his eyes and looked at Swan, and from him to Lorraine, but he did not say anything. He still had that tightened look around his mouth which spelled pain.

"Pretty quick now we get you fixed up good," Swan told him cheerfully. "One mile more is all, and we get the horses and I make a good bed for you." He looked a signal, and Lorraine once more took up the stretcher.

Another mile seemed a long way, light though Swan had made the load for her. She thought once that he must have some clairvoyant power, because whenever she felt as if her arms were breaking, Swan would tell her to stop a minute.

"How do you know a doctor will come?" she asked Swan suddenly, when they were resting with the Thurman ranch in view half a mile below them.

Swan did not look at her directly, as had been his custom. She saw a darker shade of red creep up into his cheeks. "My mother says she would send a doctor quick," he replied hesitatingly. "You will see. It is because - your father he is not like other men in this country. Your father is a good man. That is why a doctor comes."

Lorraine looked at him strangely and stooped again to her burden. She did not speak again until they were passing the Thurman fence where it ran up into the mouth of the canyon. A few horses were grazing there, the sun striking their sides with the sheen of satin. They stared curiously at the little procession, snorted and started to run, heads and tails held high. But one wheeled suddenly and came galloping toward them, stopped when he was quite close, ducked and went thundering past to the head of the field. Lorraine gave a sharp little scream and set down the stretcher with a lurch, staring after the horse wide-eyed, her face white.

"They do it for play," Swan said reassuringly. "They don't hurt you. The fence is between, and they don't hurt you anyway."

"That horse with the white face - I saw it - and when the man struck it with his quirt it went past me, running like that and dragging - *oh-h*!" She leaned against the bluff side, her face covered with her two palms.

Swan glanced down at Brit, saw that his eyes were closed, ducked his head from under the looped rope and went to Lorraine.

"The man that struck that horse - do you know that man?" he asked, all the good nature gone from his voice.

"No - I don't know - I saw him twice, by the lightning flashes. He shot - and then I saw him -" She stopped abruptly, stood for a minute longer with her eyes covered, then dropped her hands limply to her sides. But when the horse came circling back with a great flourish, she shivered and her hands closed into the fists of a fighter.

"Are you a Sawtooth man?" she demanded suddenly, looking up at Swan defiantly. "It was a nightmare. I - I dreamed once about a horse - like that."

Swan's wide-open eyes softened a little. "The Sawtooth calls me that damn Swede on Bear Top," he explained. "I took a homestead up there and some day they will want to buy my place or they will want to make a fight with me to get the water. Could you know that man again?"

"Raine!" Brit's voice held a warning, and Lorraine shivered again as she turned toward him. "Raine, you -"

He closed his eyes again, and she could get no further speech from him. But she thought she understood. He did not want her to talk about Fred Thurman. She went to her end of the stretcher and waited there while Swan put the rope over his head. They went on, Lorraine walking with her head averted, trying not to see the blaze-faced roan, trying to shut out the memory of him dashing past her with his terrible burden, that night.

Swan did not speak of the matter again. With Lorraine's assistance he carried Brit into Thurman's cabin, laid him, stretcher and all, on the bed and hurried out to catch and harness the team of work horses. Lorraine waited beside her father, helpless and miserable. There was nothing to do but wait, yet waiting seemed to her the one thing she could not do.

"Raine!" Brit's voice was very weak, but Lorraine jumped as though a trumpet had bellowed suddenly in her ear. "Swan - he's all right. But don't go telling - all yuh know and some besides. He ain't - Sawtooth, but - he might let out -"

"I know. I won't, dad. It was that horse -"

Brit turned his face to the wall as if no more was to be said on the subject. Lorraine wandered around the cabin, which was no larger than her father's place. The rooms were scrupulously clean - neater than the Quirt, she observed guiltily. Not one article, however small and unimportant, seemed to be out of its place, and the floors of both rooms were scrubbed whiter than any floors she had ever seen. Swan's housekeeping qualities made her ashamed of her own imperfections; and when, thinking that Swan must be hungry and that the least she could do was to set out food for him, she opened the cupboard, she had a swift, embarrassed vision of her own culinary imperfections. She could cook better food than her dad had been content to eat and to set before others, but Swan's bread was a triumph in sour dough. Biscuits tall and light as bread can be she found, covered neatly with a cloth. Prunes stewed so that there was not one single wrinkle in them - Lorraine could scarcely believe they were prunes until she tasted them. She was investigating a pot of beans when Swan came in.

"Food I am thinking of, Miss," he grinned at her. "We shall hurry, but it is not good to go hungry. Milk is outside in a cupboard. It is quicker than to make coffee."

"It will be dark before we can get him home," said Lorraine uneasily. "And by the time a doctor can get out there -"

"A doctor will be there, I think. You don't believe, but that is no difference to his coming just the same."

He brought the milk, poured off the creamy top into a pitcher, stirred it, and quietly insisted that she drink two glasses. Lorraine observed that Swan himself ate very little, bolting down a biscuit in great mouthfuls while he carried a mattress and blankets out to spread in the wagon. It was like his pretense of weariness on the long carry down the canyon, she thought. It was for her more than for himself that he was thinking.

## CHAPTER TWELVE

## THE QUIRT PARRIES THE FIRST BLOW

A car with dimmed lights stood in front of the Quirt cabin when Swan drove around the last low ridge and down to the gate. The rattle of the wagon must have been heard, for the door opened suddenly and Frank stood revealed in the yellow light of the kerosene lamp on the table within. Behind Frank, Lorraine saw Jim and Sorry standing in their shirt sleeves looking out into the dark. Another, shorter figure she glimpsed as Frank and the two men stepped out and came striding hastily toward them. Lorraine jumped out and ran to meet them, hoping and fearing that her hope was foolish. That car might easily be only Bob Warfield on some errand of no importance. Still, she hoped.

"That you, Raine? Where's Brit? What's all this about Brit being hurt? A doctor from Shoshone -"

"A *doctor*? Oh, did a doctor come, then? Oh, help Swan carry dad in! I'm - oh, I'm afraid he's awfully injured!"

"Yes-s - but how'n hell did a doctor know about it?" Sorry, the silent, blurted unexpectedly.

"Oh, - never mind - but get dad in. I'll -" She ran past them without finishing her sentence and burst incoherently into the presence of an extremely calm little man with gray whiskers and dust on the shoulders of his coat. These details, I may add, formed the sum of Lorraine's first impression of him.

"Well! Well!" he remonstrated with a professional briskness, when she nearly bowled him over. "We seem to be in something of a hurry! Is this the patient I was sent to examine?"

"No!" Lorraine flashed impatiently over her shoulder as she rushed into her own room and began turning down the covers. "It's dad, of course - and you'd better get your coat off and get ready to go to work, because I expect he's just one mass of broken bones!"

The doctor smiled behind his whiskers and returned to the doorway to direct the carrying in of his patient. His sharp eyes went immediately to Brit's face, pallid under the leathery tan, his fingers went to Brit's hairy, corded wrist. The doctor smiled no more that evening.

"No, he is not a mass of broken bones, I am happy to say," he reported gravely to Lorraine afterwards. "He has a sufficient number, however. The left scapula is fractured, likewise the clavicle, and there is a compound fracture of the femur. There is some injury to the head, the exact extent of which I cannot as yet determine. He should be removed to a hospital, unless you are prepared to have a nurse here for some time, or to assume the burden of a long and tedious illness." He looked at her thoughtfully. "The journey to Shoshone would be a considerable strain on the patient in his present condition. He has a splendid amount of constitutional vitality, or he would scarcely have survived his injuries so long without medical attendance. Can you tell me just how the accident occurred?"

"Excuse me, doctor - and Miss," Swan diffidently interrupted. "I could ask you to take a look on my shoulder, if you please. If you are done setting bones in Mr. Hunter. I have a great pain on my shoulder from carrying so long."

"You never mentioned it!" Lorraine reproached him quickly. "Of course it must be looked after right away. And then, Doctor, I'd like to talk to you, if you don't mind." She watched them retreat to the bunk-house together, Swan's big form towering above the doctor's slighter figure. Swan was talking earnestly, the mumble of his voice reaching Lorraine without the enunciation of any particular word to give a clue to what he was saying. But it struck her that his voice did not sound quite natural; not so Swedish, not so careful.

Frank came tiptoeing out of the room where Brit lay bandaged and unconscious and stood close to Lorraine, looking down at her solemnly.

"How 'n 'ell did he git here - the doctor?" he demanded, making a great effort to hold his voice down to a whisper, and forgetting now and then. "How'd *he* know Brit rolled off'n the grade? Us here, *we* never knowed it, and I was tryin' to send him back when you came. He said somebody telephoned there was a man hurt in a runaway. There ain't a telephone closer'n the Sawtooth, and that there's a good twenty mile and more from where Brit was hurt. It's damn funny."

"Yes, it is," Lorraine admitted uncomfortably. "I don't know any more than you do about it."

"Well, how'n 'ell did it happen? Brit, he oughta know enough to rough-lock down that hill. An' that team ain't a runaway team. *I* never had no trouble with 'em - they're good at holdin' a load. They'll set down an' slide but what they'll hold 'er. What become of the horses?"

"Why - they're over there yet. We forgot all about the horses, I think. Caroline was standing up, all right. The other horse may be killed. I don't know - it was lying down. And Yellowjacket was up that little gully just this side of the wreck, when I left him. They did try to hold the load, Frank. Something must have happened to the brake. I saw dad crawling out from under the wagon just before I got to where the load was standing. Or some one did. I think it was dad. But Caroline kicked my horse down off the road, and I only saw him a minute - but it *must* have been dad. And then, a little way down the hill, something went wrong."

Frank seemed trying to reconstruct the accident from Lorraine's description. "He'd no business to start down if his rough-lock wasn't all right," he said. "It ain't like him. Brit's careful about them things - little men most always are. I don't see how 'n 'ell it worked loose. It's a damn queer layout all around; and this here doctor gitting here ahead of you folks, that there is the queerest. What's he say about Brit? Think he'll pull through?"

The doctor himself, coming up just then, answered the question. Of course the patient would pull through! What were doctors for? As to his reason for coming, he referred them to Mr. Vjolmar, whom he thought could better explain the matter.

The three of them waited, - five of them, since Jim and Sorry had come up, anxious to hear the doctor's opinion and anything else pertaining to the affair. Swan was coming slowly from the bunkhouse, buttoning his coat. He seemed to feel that they were waiting for him and to know why. His manner was diffident, deprecating even.

"We may as well go in out of the mosquitoes," the doctor suggested. "And I wish you would tell these people what you told me, young man. Don't be afraid to speak frankly; it is rather amazing but not at all impossible, as I can testify. In fact," he added dryly, "my presence here ought to settle any doubt of that. Just tell them, young man, about your mother."

Swan was the last to enter the kitchen, and he stood leaning against the closed door, turning his old hat round and round, his eyes going swiftly from face to face. They were watching him, and Swan blushed a deep red while he told them about his mother in Boise, and how he could talk to her with his thoughts. He explained laboriously how the thoughts from her came like his mother speaking in his head, and that his thoughts reached her in the same way. He said that since he was a little boy they could talk together with their thoughts, but people laughed and some called them crazy, so that now he did not like to have somebody know that he could do it.

"But Brit Hunter's hurt bad, so a doctor must come quick, or I think he maybe will die. It takes too long to ride a horse to Echo from this ranch, so I call on my mother, and I tell my mother a doctor must come quick to this ranch. So my mother sends a telephone to this doctor in Shoshone, and he comes. That is all. But I would not like it if everybody maybe finds it out that I do that, and makes talk about it."

He looked straight at Jim and Sorry, and those two unprepossessing ones looked at each other and at Swan and at the doctor and at each other again, and headed for the door. But Swan was leaning against it, and his eyes were on them. "I would like it if you say somebody rides to get the doctor," he hinted quietly.

Sorry looked at Jim. "I rode like hell," he stated heavily. "I leave it to Jim."

"You shore'n hell did!" Jim agreed, and Swan removed his big form from the door.

"You boys goin' over t' Spirit Canyon?" Frank wanted to know.

"Yeah," said Sorry, answering for them both, and they went out, giving Swan a sidelong look of utter bafflement as they passed him. Talking by the thought route from Spirit Canyon to Boise City was evidently a bit too much for even their phlegmatic souls to contemplate with perfect calm.

"They'll keep it to theirselves, whether they believe it or not," Frank assured Swan in his labored whisper. "It don't go down with me. I ain't supe'stitious enough fer that."

"The doctor he comes, don't he?" Swan retorted. "I shall go back now and milk the cows and do chores."

"But if your shoulder is lame, Swan, how can you?" Lorraine asked in her unexpected fashion.

Swan swallowed and looked helplessly at the doctor, who stood smoothing his chin. "The muscle strain is not serious," he said calmly. "A little gentle exercise will prevent further trouble, I think." Whereupon he turned abruptly to the door of the other room, glanced in at Brit and beckoned Lorraine with an upraised finger.

"You have had a hard time of it yourself, young lady," he told her. "You needn't worry about Swan. He is not suffering appreciably. I shall mix you a very unpleasant dose of medicine, and then I want you to go to bed and sleep. I shall stay with your father to-night; not that it is necessary, but because I prefer daylight for the trip back to town. So there is no reason why you should sit up and wear yourself out. You will have plenty of time to do that while your father's bones mend."

He proceeded to mix the unpleasant dose, which Lorraine swallowed and straightway forgot, in the muddle of thoughts that whirled confusingly in her brain. Little things distressed her oddly, while her father's desperate state left her numb. She lay down on the cot in the farther corner of the kitchen where her father had slept just last night - it seemed so long ago! - and almost immediately, as her senses recorded it, bright sunlight was shining into the room.

## CHAPTER THIRTEEN

## LONE TAKES HIS STAND

Lone Morgan, over at Elk Spring camp, was just sitting down to eat his midday meal when some one shouted outside. Lone stiffened in his chair, felt under his coat, and then got up with some deliberation and looked out of the window before he went to the door. All this was a matter of habit, bred of Lone's youth in the feud country, and had nothing whatever to do with his conscience.

"Hello!" he called, standing in the doorway and grinning a welcome to Swan, who stood with one arm resting on the board gate. "She's on the table - come on in."

"I don't know if you're home with the door shut like that," Swan explained, coming up to the cabin. "I chased a coyote from Rock City to here, and by golly, he's going yet! I'll get him sometime, maybe. He's smart, but you can beat anything with thinking if you don't stop thinking. Always the other feller stops sometimes, and then you get him. You believe that?"

"It most generally works out that way," Lone admitted, getting another plate and cup from the cupboard, which was merely a box nailed with its bottom to the wall, and a flour sack tacked across the front for a curtain. "Even a coyote slips up now and then, I reckon."

Swan sat down, smoothing his tousled yellow hair with both

hands as he did so. "By golly, my shoulder is sore yet from carrying Brit Hunter," he remarked carelessly, flexing his muscles and grimacing a little.

Lone was pouring the coffee, and he ran Swan's cup over before he noticed what he was doing. Swan looked up at him and looked away again, reaching for a cloth to wipe the spilled coffee from the table.

"How was that?" Lone asked, turning away to the stove. "What-all happened to Brit Hunter?"

Swan, with his plate filled and his coffee well sweetened, proceeded to relate with much detail the story of Brit's misfortune. "By golly, I don't see how he don't get killed," he finished, helping himself to another biscuit. "By *golly*, I don't. Falling into Spirit Canyon is like getting dragged by a horse. It should kill a man. What you think, Lone?"

"It didn't, you say." Lone's eyes were turned to his coffee cup.

"It don't kill Brit Hunter - not yet. I think maybe he dies with all his bones broke, like that. By golly, that shows you what could happen if a man don't think. Brit should look at that chain on his wheel before he starts down that road."

"Oh. His brake didn't hold, eh?"

"I look at that wagon," Swan answered carefully. "It is something funny about that chain. I worked hauling logs in the mountains, once. It is something damn funny about that chain, the way it's fixed."

Lone did not ask him for particulars, as perhaps Swan expected. He did not speak at all for awhile, but presently pushed back his plate as if his appetite were gone.

"It's like Fred Thurman," Swan continued moralizing. "If Fred don't ride backwards, I bet he don't get killed - like that."

"Where's Brit now?" Lone asked, getting up and putting on his hat. "At the ranch?"

"Or heaven, maybe," Swan responded sententiously. "But my dog Yack, he don't howl yet. I guess Brit's at the ranch."

"Sorry I'm busy to-day," said Lone, opening the door. "You stay as long as you like, Swan. I've got some riding to do."

"I'll wash the dishes, and then I maybe will think quicker than that coyote. I'm after him, by golly, till I get him."

Lone muttered something and went out. Within five minutes Swan, hearing hoofbeats, looked out through a crack in the door and saw Lone riding at a gallop along the trail to Rock City. "Good bait. He swallows the hook," he commented to himself, and his good-natured grin was not brightening his face while he washed the dishes and tidied the cabin.

With Lone rode bitterness of soul and a sick fear that had nothing to do with his own destiny. How long ago Brit had been hurled into the canyon Lone did not know; he had not asked. But he judged that it must have been very recently. Swan had not told him of anything but the runaway, and of helping to carry Brit home - and of the "damn funny thing about the chain" - the rough-lock, he must have meant. Too well Lone understood the sinister meaning that probably lay behind that phrase.

"They've started on the Quirt now," he told himself with foreboding. "She's been telling her father -"

Lone fell into bitter argument with himself. Just how far was it justifiable to mind his own business? And if he did not mind it, what possible chance had he against a power so ruthless and so cunning? An accident to a man driving a loaded wagon down the Spirit Canyon grade had a diabolic plausibility that no man in the country could question. Brit, he reasoned, could not have known before he started that his rough-lock had been tampered with, else he would have fixed it. Neither was Brit the man to forget the brake on his load. If Brit lived, he might talk as much as he pleased, but he could never prove that his accident had been deliberately staged with murderous intent.

Lone lifted his head and looked away across the empty miles of sageland to the quiet blue of the mountains beyond. Peace - the peace of untroubled wilderness - brooded over the land. Far in the distance, against the rim of rugged hills, was an irregular splotch of brown which was the headquarters of the Sawtooth. Lone turned his wrist to the right, and John Doe, obeying the rein signal, left the trail and began picking his way stiff-legged down the steep slope of the ridge, heading directly toward the home ranch.

John Doe was streaked with sweat and his flanks were palpitating with fatigue when Lone rode up to the corral and dismounted. Pop Bridgers saw him and came bow-legging eagerly forward with gossip titillating on his meddlesome tongue, but Lone stalked by him with only a surly nod. Bob Warfield he saw at a distance and gave no sign of recognition. He met Hawkins coming down from his house and stopped in the trail.

"Have you got time to go back to the office and fix up my time, Hawkins?" he asked without prelude. "I'm quitting to-day."

Hawkins stared and named the Biblical place of torment. "What yuh quittin' for, Lone?" he added incredulously. "All you boys got a raise last month; ain't that good enough?"

"Plenty good enough, so long as I work for the outfit."

"Well, what's wrong? You've been with us five years, Lone, and it's suited you all right so far -"

Lone looked at him. "Say, I never set out to *marry* the Sawtooth," he stated calmly. "And if I have married you-all by accident, you can get a bill of divorce for desertion. This ain't the first time a man ever quit yuh, is it, Hawkins?"

"No - and there ain't a man on the pay roll we can't do without," Hawkins retorted, his neck stiffening with resentment. "It's a kinda rusty trick, though, Lone, quittin' without notice and leaving a camp empty."

"Elk Spring won't run away," Lone assured him without emotion. "She's been left alone a week or two at a time during roundups. I don't reckon the outfit'll bust up before you get a man down there."

The foreman looked at him curiously, for this was not like Lone, whose tone had always been soft and friendly, and whose manner had no hint of brusqueness. There was a light, too, in Lone's eyes that had not been there before. But Hawkins would not question him further. If Lone Morgan or any other man wanted to quit, that was his privilege, - providing, of course, that his leaving was not likely to menace the peace and security of the Sawtooth. Lone had made it a point to mind his own business, always. He had never asked questions, he had never surmised or gossiped. So Hawkins gave him a check for his wages and let him go with no more than a foreman's natural reluctance to lose a trustworthy man.

By hard riding along short cuts, Lone reached the Quirt ranch and dropped reins at the doorstep, not much past mid-afternoon.

"I rode over to see if there's anything I can do," he said, when Lorraine opened the door to him. He did not like to ask about her father, fearing that the news would be bad.

"Why, thank you for coming." Lorraine stepped back, tacitly inviting him to enter. "Dad knows us to-day, but of course he's terribly hurt and can't talk much. We do need some one to go to town for things. Frank helps me with dad, and Jim and Sorry are trying to keep things going on the ranch. And Swan does what he can, of course, but -"

"I just thought you maybe needed somebody right bad," said Lone quietly, meaning a great deal more than Lorraine dreamed that he meant. "I'm not doing anything at all, right now, so I can just as well help out as not. I can go to town right away, if I can borrow a horse. John Doe, he's pretty tired. I been pushing him right through - not knowing there was a town trip ahead of him."

Lorraine found her eyes going misty. He was so quiet, and so reassuring in his quiet. Half her burden seemed to slip from her shoulders while she looked at him. She turned away, groping for the door latch.

"You may see dad, if you like, while I get the list of things the doctor ordered. He left only a little while ago, and I was waiting for one of the boys to come back so I could send him to town."

It was on Lone's tongue to ask why the doctor had not taken in the order himself and instructed some one to bring out the things; but he remembered how very busy with its own affairs was Echo and decided that the doctor was wise.

He tiptoed in to the bed and saw a sallow face covered with stubbly gray whiskers and framed with white bandages. Brit opened his eyes and moved his thin lips in some kind of greeting, and Lone sat down on the edge of a chair, feeling as miserably guilty as if he himself had brought the old man to this pass. It seemed to him that Brit must know more of the accident than Swan had told, and the thought did not add to his comfort. He waited until Brit opened his eyes again, and then he leaned forward, holding Brit's wandering glance with his own intent gaze.

"I ain't working now," he said, lowering his voice so that Lorraine could not hear. "So I'm going to stay here and help see you through with this. I've quit the Sawtooth."

Brit's eyes cleared and studied Lone's face. "D'you know - anything?"

"No, I don't." Lone's face hardened a little. "But I wanted you to know that I'm - with the Quirt, now."

"Frank hire yuh?"

"No. I ain't hired at all. I'm just - *with* yuh."

"We - need yuh," said Brit grimly, looking Lone straight in the eyes.

## CHAPTER FOURTEEN

## "FRANK'S DEAD"

"Frank come yet?" The peevish impatience of an invalid whose horizon has narrowed to his own personal welfare and wants was in Brit's voice. Two weeks he had been sick, and his temper had not sweetened with the pain of his broken bones and the enforced idleness. Brit was the type of man who is never quiet unless he is asleep or too ill to get out of bed.

Lorraine came to the doorway and looked in at him. Two weeks had set their mark on her also. She seemed older, quieter in her ways; there were shadows in her eyes and a new seriousness in the set of her mouth. She had had her burdens, and she had borne them with more patience than many an older woman would have done, but what she thought of those burdens she did not say.

"No, dad - but I thought I heard a wagon a little while ago. He must be coming," she said.

"Where's Lone at?" Brit moved restlessly on the pillow and twisted his face at the pain.

"Lone isn't back, either."

"He ain't? Where'd he go?"

Lorraine came to the bedside and, lifting Brit's head carefully, arranged the pillow as she knew he liked it. "I don't know where he went," she said dully. "He rode off just after dinner. Do you want your supper now? Or would you rather wait until Frank brings the fruit?"

"I'd ruther wait - if Frank don't take all night," Brit grumbled. "I hope he ain't connected up with that Echo booze. If he has -"

"Oh, no, dad! Don't borrow trouble. Frank was anxious to get home as soon as he could. He'll be coming any minute, now. I'll go listen for the wagon."

"No use listenin'. You couldn't hear it in that sand - not till he gits to the gate. I don't see where Lone goes to, all the time. Where's Jim and Sorry, then?"

"Oh, they've had their supper and gone to the bunk-house. Do you want them?"

"No! What'd I want 'em fur? Not to look at, that's sure. I want to know how things is going on this ranch. And from all I can make out, they ain't goin' at all," Brit fretted. "What was you 'n Lone talkin' so long about, out in the kitchen last night? Seems to me you 'n' him have got a lot to say to each other, Raine."

"Why, nothing in particular. We were just - talking. We're all human beings, dad; we have to talk sometimes. There's nothing else to do."

"Well, I caught something about the Sawtooth. I don't want you talking to Lone or anybody else about that outfit, Raine. I told yuh so once. He's all right - I ain't saying anything against Lone - but the less you have to say the more you'll have to be thankful fur, mebby."

"I was wondering if Swan could have gotten word somehow to the Sawtooth and had them telephone out that you were hurt. And Lone was drawing a map of the trails and showing me how far it was from the canyon to the Sawtooth ranch. And he was asking me just how it happened that the brake didn't hold, and I said it must have been all right, because I saw you come out from under the wagon just before you hitched up. I thought you were fixing the chain on them."

"Huh?" Brit lifted his head off the pillow and let it drop back again, because of the pain in his shoulder. "You never seen me crawl out from under no wagon. I come straight down the hill to the team."

"Well, I saw some one. He went up into the brush. I thought it was you." Lorraine turned in the doorway and stood looking at him erplexedly. "We shouldn't be talking about it, dad - the doctor said we mustn't. But are you *sure* it wasn't you? Because I certainly saw a man crawl out from under the wagon and start up the hill. Then the horses acted up, and I couldn't see him after Yellowjacket jumped off the road."

Brit lay staring up at the ceiling, apparently unheeding her explanation. Lorraine watched him for a minute and returned to the kitchen door, peering out and listening for Frank to come from Echo with supplies and the mail and, more important just now, fresh fruit for her father.

"I think he's coming, dad," she called in to her father. "I just heard something down by the gate."

She could save a few minutes, she thought, by running down to the corral where Frank would probably stop and unload the few sacks of grain he was bringing, before he drove up to the house. Frank was very methodical in a fussy, purposeless way, she had observed. Twice he had driven to Echo since her father had been hurt, and each time he had stopped at the corral on his way to the house. So she closed the screen door behind her, careful that it should not slam, and ran down the path in the heavy dusk wherein crickets were rasping a strident chorus.

"Oh! It's you, is it, Lone?" she exclaimed, when she neared the vague figure of a man unsaddling a horse. "You didn't see Frank coming anywhere, did you? Dad won't have his supper until

Frank comes with the things I sent for. He's late."

Lone was lifting the saddle off the back of John Doe, which he had bought from the Sawtooth because he was fond of the horse. He hesitated and replaced the saddle, pulling the blanket straight under it.

"I saw him coming an hour ago," he said. "I was back up on the ridge, and I saw a team turn into the Quirt trail from the ford. It couldn't be anybody but Frank. I'll ride out and meet him."

He was mounted and gone before she realized that he was ready. She heard the sharp staccato of John Doe's hoofbeats and wondered why Lone had not waited for another word from her. It was as if she had told him that Frank was in some terrible danger, - yet she had merely complained that he was late. The bunk-house door opened, and Sorry came out on the doorstep, stood there a minute and came slowly to meet her as she retraced her steps to the house.

"Where'd Lone go so sudden?" he asked, when she came close to him in the dusk. "That was him, wasn't it?"

Lorraine stopped and stood looking at him without speaking. A vague terror had seized her. She wanted to scream, and yet she could think of nothing to scream over. It was Lone's haste, she told herself impatiently. Her nerves were ragged from nursing her dad and from worrying over things she must not talk about, - that forbidden subject which never left her mind for long.

"Wasn't that him?" Sorry repeated uneasily. "What took him off again in such a rush?"

"Oh, I don't know! He said Frank should have been here long ago. He went to look for him. Sorry," she cried suddenly, "what *is* the matter with this place? I feel as if something horrible was just ready to jump out at us all. I - I want my back against something solid, all the time, so that nothing can creep up behind. Nothing," she added desperately, "could happen to Frank between here and the turn-off at the ford, could it? Lone saw him turn into our trail over an hour ago, he said."

Sorry, his fingers thrust into his overalls pockets, his thumbs hooked over the waistband, spat into the sand beside the path. "Well, he started off with a cracked doubletree," he said slowly. "He mighta busted 'er pullin' through that sand hollow. She was wired up pretty good, though, and there was more wire in the rig. I don't know of anything else that'd be liable to happen, unless -"

"Unless what?" Lorraine prompted sharply. "There's too much that isn't talked about, on this ranch. What else could happen?"

Sorry edged away from her. "Well - I dunno as anything would be liable to happen," he said uncomfortably. "'Taint likely him 'n' Brit 'd both have accidents - not right hand-runnin'."

"*Accidents*?" Lorraine felt her throat squeeze together. "Sorry, you don't mean - Sawtooth accidents?" she blurted.

She surprised a grunt out of Sorry, who looked over his shoulder as if he feared eavesdroppers. "Where'd you git that idee?" he demanded. "I dunno what you mean. Ain't that yore dad callin' yuh?"

Lorraine ignored the hint. "You *do* know what I mean. Why did you say they wouldn't both be likely to have accidents hand-running? And why don't you *do* something? Why does every one just keep still and let things happen, and not say a word? If there's any chance of Frank having an - an *accident*, I should think you'd be out looking after him, and not standing there with your hands in your pockets just waiting to see if he shows up or if he doesn't show up. You're all just like these rabbits out in the sage. You'll hide under a bush and wait until you're almost stepped on before you so much as wiggle an ear! I'm getting good and tired of this meek business!"

"We-ell," Sorry drawled amiably as she went past him, "playin' rabbit-under-a-bush mebby don't look purty, but it's dern good life insurance."

"A coward's policy," Lorraine taunted him over her shoulder, and went to see what her father wanted. When he, too, wanted to know why Lone had come and gone again in such a hurry, Lorraine felt all the courage go out of her at once. Their very uneasiness seemed to prove that there was more than enough cause for it. Yet, when she forced herself to stop and think, it was all about nothing. Frank had driven to Echo and had not returned exactly on time, though a dozen things might have detained him.

She was listening at the door when Swan appeared unexpectedly before her, having walked over from the Thurman ranch after doing the chores. To him she observed that Frank was an hour late, and Swan, whistling softly to Jack - Lorraine was surprised to hear how closely the call resembled the chirp of a bird - strode away without so much as a pretense at excuse. Lorraine stared after him wide-eyed, wondering and yet not daring to wonder.

Her father called to her fretfully, and she went in to him again and told him what Sorry had said about the cracked doubletree, and persuaded him to let her bring his supper at once, and to have the fruit later when Frank arrived. Brit did not say much, but she sensed his uneasiness, and her own increased in proportion. Later she saw two tiny, glowing points down by the corral and knew that Sorry and Jim were down there, waiting and listening, ready to do whatever was needed of them; although what that would be she could not even conjecture.

She made her father comfortable, chattered aimlessly to combat her understanding of his moody silence, and listened and waited and tried her pitiful best not to think that anything could be wrong. The subdued chuckling of the wagon in the sand outside the gate startled her with its unmistakable reality after so many false impressions that she heard it.

"Frank's coming, dad," she announced relievedly, "and I'll go and get the mail and the fruit."

She ran down the path again, almost light-hearted in her relief from that vague terror which had held her for the past hour. From the corral Sorry and Jim came walking up the path to meet the wagon which was making straight for the bunk-house instead of going first to the stable. One man rode on the seat, driving the team which walked slowly, oddly, reminding Lorraine of a funeral procession. Beside the wagon rode Lone, his head drooped a little in the starlight. It was not until the team stopped before the bunk-house that Lorraine knew what it was that gave her that strange, creepy feeling of disaster. It was not Frank Johnson, but Swan Vjolmar who climbed limberly down from the seat without speaking and turned toward the back of the wagon.

"Why, where's Frank?" she asked, going up to where Lone was dismounting in silence.

"He's there - in the wagon. We picked him up back here about three-quarters of a mile or so."

"What's the matter? Is he drunk?" This was Sorry who came up to Swan and stood ready to lend a hand.

"He's so drunk he falls out of wagon down the road, but he don't have whisky smell by his face," was Swan's ambiguous reply.

"He's not hurt, is he?" Lorraine pressed close, and felt a hand on her arm pulling her gently away.

"He's hurt," Lone said, just behind her. "We'll take him into the bunk-house and bring him to. Run along to the house and don't worry - and don't say anything to your dad, either. There's no need to bother him about it. We'll look after Frank."

Already Swan and Sorry and Jim were lifting Frank's limp form from the rear of the wagon. It sagged in their arms like a dead thing, and Lorraine stepped back shuddering as they passed her. A minute later she followed them inside, where Jim was lighting the lamp with shaking fingers. By the glow of the match Lorraine saw how sober Jim looked, how his chin was trembling under the drooping, sandy mustache. She stared at him, hating to read the emotion in his heavy face that she had always thought so utterly void of feeling.

"It isn't - he isn't -" she began, and turned upon Swan, who was beside the bunk, looking down at Frank's upturned face. "Swan, if it's serious enough for a doctor, can't you send another thought message to your mother?" she asked. "He looks - oh, Lone! He isn't *dead*, is he?"

Swan turned his head and stared down at her, and from her face his glance went sharply to Lone's downcast face. He looked again at Lorraine.

"To-night I can't talk with my mind," Swan told her bluntly. "Not always I can do that. I could ask Lone how can a man be drunk so he falls off the wagon when no whisky smell is on his breath."

"Breath? Hell! There ain't no breath to smell," Sorry exclaimed as unexpectedly as his speeches usually were. "If he's breathin' I can't tell it on him."

"He's got to be breathing!" Lone declared with a suppressed fierceness that made them all look at him. "I found a half bottle of whisky in his pocket - but Swan's right. There wasn't a smell of it on his breath - I tell you now, boys, that he was lying in the sand between two sagebushes, on his face. And there is where he got the blow - *behind his ear*. It's one of them accidents that you've got to figure out for yourself."

"Oh, do something!" Lorraine cried distractedly. "Never mind now how it happened, or whether he was drunk or not - bring him to his senses first, and let him explain. If there's whisky, wouldn't that help if he swallowed some now? And there's medicine for dad's bruises in the house. I'll get it. And Swan! Won't you *please* talk to your mother and tell her we need the doctor?"

Swan drew back. "I can't," he said shortly. "Better you send to Echo for telegraph. And if you have medicine, it should be on his head quick."

Lone was standing with his fingers pressed on Frank's wrist. He looked up, hesitated, drew out his knife and opened the small blade. He moved so that his back was to Lorraine, and still holding the wrist he made a small, clean cut in the flesh. The three others stooped, stared with tightened lips at the bloodless incision, straightened and looked at one another dumbly.

"I'd like to lie to you," Lone told Lorraine, speaking over his shoulder. "But I won't. You're too game and too square. Go and stay with your dad, but don't let him know - get him to sleep. We don't need that medicine, nor a doctor either. Frank's dead. I reckon he was dead when he hit the ground."

## CHAPTER FIFTEEN

## SWAN TRAILS A COYOTE

At daybreak Swan was striding toward the place where Frank Johnson had been found. Lone, his face moody, his eyes clouded with thought, rode beside him, while Jack trotted loose-jointedly at Swan's heels. Swan had his rifle, and Lone's six-shooter showed now and then under his coat when the wind flipped back a corner. Neither had spoken since they left the ranch, where Jim was wandering dismally here and there, trying to do the chores when his heart was heavy with a sense of personal loss and grim foreboding. None save Brit had slept during the night - and Brit had slept only because Lorraine had prudently given him a full dose of the sedative left by the doctor for that very purpose. Sorry had gone to Echo to send a telegram to the coroner, and he was likely to return now at any time. Wherefore Swan and Lone were going to look over the ground before others had trampled out what evidence there might be in the shape of footprints.

They reached the spot where the team had stopped of its own accord in crossing a little, green meadow, and had gone to feeding. Lone pulled up and half turned in the saddle, looking at Swan questioningly.

"Is that dog of yours any good at trailing?" he asked abruptly. "I've got a theory that somebody was in that wagon with Frank, and drove on a ways before he jumped out. I believe if you'd put that dog on the trail -"

"If I put that dog on the trail he stays on the trail all day, maybe," Swan averred with some pride. "By golly, he follows a coyote till he drops."

"Well, it's a coyote we're after now," said Lone. "A sheep-killer that has made his last killin'. Right here's where I rode up and caught the team, last night. We better take a look along here for tracks."

Swan stared at him curiously, but he did not speak, and the two went on more slowly, their glances roving here and there along the trail edge, looking for footprints. Once the dog Jack swung off the trail into the brush, and Swan followed him while Lone stopped and awaited the result. Swan came back presently, with Jack sulking at his heels.

"Yack, he take up the trail of a coyote," Swan explained, "but it's got the four legs, and Yack, he don't understand me when I don't follow. He thinks I'm crazy this morning."

"I reckon the team came on toward home after the fellow jumped out," Lone observed. "He'd plan that way, seems to me. I know I would."

"I guess that's right. I don't have experience in killing somebody," Swan returned blandly, and Lone was too preoccupied to wonder at the unaccustomed sarcasm.

A little farther along Swan swooped down upon a blue dotted handkerchief of the kind which men find so useful where laundries are but a name. Again Lone stopped and bent to examine it as Swan spread it out in his hands. A few tiny grains of sandstone rattled out, and in the center was a small blood spot. Swan looked up straight into Lone's dark, brooding eyes.

"By golly, Lone, you would do that, too, if you kill somebody," he began in a new tone, - the tone which Lorraine had heard indistinctly in the bunk-house when Swan was talking to the doctor. "Do you think I'm a damn fool, just because I'm a Swede?

You are smart - you think out every little thing. But you make a big mistake if you don't think some one else may be using his brain, too. This handkerchief I have seen you pull from your pocket too many times. And it had a rock in it last night, and the blood shows that it was used to hit Frank behind the ear. You think it all out - but maybe I've been thinking too. Now you're under arrest. Just stay on your horse - he can't run faster than a bullet, and I don't miss coyotes when I shoot them on the run."

"The hell you say!" Lone stared at him. "Where's your authority, Swan?"

Swan lifted the rifle to a comfortable, firing position, the muzzle pointing straight at Lone's chest. With his left hand he turned back his coat and disclosed a badge pinned to the lining.

"I'm a United States Marshal, that's all; a government hunter," he stated. "I'm hot on the trail of coyotes - all kinds. Throw that six-shooter over there in the brush, will you?"

"I hate to get the barrel all sanded up," Lone objected mildly. "You can pack it, can't you?" He grinned a little as he handed out the gun, muzzle toward himself. "You're playing safe, Swan, but if that dog of yours is any good, you'll have a change of heart pretty quick. Isn't that a man's track, just beside that flat rock? Put the dog on, why don't you?"

"Yack is on already," Swan pointed out. "Ride ahead of me, Lone."

With a shrug of his shoulders Lone obeyed, following the dog as it trotted through the brush on the trail of a man's footprints which Swan had shown it. A man might have had some trouble in keeping to the trail, but Jack trotted easily along and never once seemed at fault. In a very few minutes he stopped in a rocky depression where a horse had been tied, and waited for Swan, wagging his tail and showing his teeth in a panting smile. The man he had trailed had mounted and ridden toward the ridge to the west. Swan examined the tracks, and Lone sat on his horse

The Quirt

watching him.

Jack picked up the trail where the horseman had walked away toward the road, and Swan followed him, motioning Lone to ride ahead.

"You could tell me about this, I think, but I can find out for myself," he observed, glancing at Lone briefly.

"Sure, you can find out, if you use your eyes and do a little thinking," Lone replied. "I hope you do lay the evidence on the right doorstep."

"I will," Swan promised, looking ahead to where Jack was nosing his way through the sagebrush.

They brought up at the edge of the road nearly a quarter of a mile nearer Echo than the place where Frank's body had been found. They saw where the man had climbed into the wagon, and followed to where they had found Frank beside the road, lying just as he had pitched forward from the wagon seat.

"I think," said Swan quietly, "we will go now and find out where that horse went last night."

"A good idea," Lone agreed. "Do you see how it was done, Swan? When he saw the team coming, away back toward Echo, he rode down into that wash and tied his horse. He was walking when Frank overtook him, I reckon - maybe claiming his horse had broke away from him. He had a rock in his handkerchief. Frank stopped and gave him a lift, and he used the rock first chance he got. Then I reckon he stuck the whisky bottle in Frank's pocket and heaved him out. He dropped the handkerchief out of his hip pocket when he jumped out of the rig. It's right simple, and if folks didn't get to wondering about it, it'd be safe as any killing can be. As safe," he added meaningly, "as dragging Fred Thurman, or unhooking Brit's chain-lock before he started down the canyon with his load of posts."

Swan did not answer, but turned back to where the horse had been left tied and took up the trail from there. As before, the dog trotted along, Lone riding close behind him and Swan striding after. They did not really need the dog, for the hoofprints were easily followed for the greater part of the way.

They had gone perhaps four miles when Lone turned, resting a hand on the cantle of his saddle while he looked back at Swan. "You see where he was headed for, don't yuh, Swan?" he asked, his tone as friendly as though he was not under arrest as a murderer. "If he didn't go to Whisper, I'll eat my hat."

"You're the man to know," Swan retorted grimly. And then, because Lone's horse had slowed in a long climb over a ridge, he came up even with a stirrup. "Lone, I hate to do it. I'd like you, if you don't kill for a living. But for that I could shoot you quick as a coyote. You're smart - but not smart enough. You gave yourself away when I showed you Fred's saddle. After that I knew who was the Sawtooth killer that I came here to find."

"You thought you knew," Lone corrected calmly.

"You don't have to lie," Swan informed him bluntly. "You don't have to tell anything. I find out for myself if I make mistake."

"Go to it," Lone advised him coldly. "It don't make a darn bit of difference to me whether I ride in front of you or behind. I'm so glad you're here on the job, Swan, that I'm plumb willing to be tied hand and foot if it'll help you any."

"When a man's too damn willing to be my prisoner," Swan observed seriously, "he gets tied, all right. Put out your hands, Lone. You look good to me with bracelets on, when you talk so willing to go to jail for murder."

He had slipped the rifle butt to the ground, and before Lone quite realized what he was doing Swan had a short, wicked-looking automatic pistol in one hand and a pair of handcuffs in the other. Lone flushed, but there was nothing to do but hold out his hands.

## CHAPTER SIXTEEN

## THE SAWTOOTH SHOWS ITS HAND

In her fictitious West Lorraine had long since come to look upon violence as a synonym for picturesqueness; murder and mystery were inevitably an accompaniment of chaps and spurs. But when a man she had cooked breakfast for, had talked with just a few hours ago, lay dead in the bunk-house, she forgot that it was merely an expected incident of Western life. She lay in her bed shaking with nervous dread, and the shrill rasping of the crickets and tree-toads was unendurable.

After the first shock had passed a deep, fighting rage filled her, made her long for day so that she might fight back somehow. Who was the Sawtooth Company, that they could sweep human beings from their path so ruthlessly and never be called to account? Not once did she doubt that this was the doing of the Sawtooth, another carefully planned "accident" calculated to rid the country of another man who in some fashion had become inimical to their interests.

From Lone she had learned a good deal about the new irrigation project which lay very close to the Sawtooth's heart. She could see how the Quirt ranch, with its water rights and its big, fertile meadows and its fences and silent disapprobation of the Sawtooth's methods, might be looked upon as an obstacle which they would be glad to remove.

That her father had been sent down that grade with a brake

deliberately made useless was a horrible thought which she could not put from her mind. She had thought and thought until it seemed to her that she knew exactly how and why the killer's plans had gone awry. She was certain that she and Swan had prevented him from climbing down into the canyon and making sure that her dad did not live to tell what mischance had overtaken him. He had probably been watching while she and Swan made that stretcher and carried her dad away out of his reach. He would not shoot *her*, - he would not dare. Nor would he dare come to the cabin and finish the job he had begun. But he had managed to kill Frank - poor old Frank, who would never grumble and argue over little things again.

There was nothing picturesque, nothing adventurous about it. It was just straight, heart-breaking tragedy, that had its sordid side too. Her dad was a querulous sick man absorbed by his sufferings and not yet out of danger, if she read the doctor's face aright. Jim and Sorry had taken orders all their life, and they would not be able to handle the ranch work alone; yet how else would it be done? There was Lone, - instinctively she turned her thoughts to him for comfort. Lone would stay and help, and somehow it would be managed.

But to think that these things could be done without fear of retribution. Jim and Sorry, Swan and Lone had not attempted to hide their belief that the Sawtooth was responsible for Frank's death, yet not one of them had hinted at the possibility of calling the sheriff, or placing the blame where it belonged. They seemed brow-beaten into the belief that it would be useless to fight back. They seemed to look upon the doings of the Sawtooth as an act of Providence, like being struck by lightning or freezing to death, as men sometimes did in that country.

To Lorraine that passive submission was the most intolerable part, the one thing she could not, would not endure. Had she lived all of her life on the Quirt, she probably would never have thought of fighting back and would have accepted conditions just as her dad seemed to accept them. But her mimic West had taught her that women sometimes dared where the men had hesitated. It never occurred to her that she should submit to the inevitable just because the men appeared to do so.

Wherefore it was a new Lorraine who rose at daybreak and silently cooked breakfast for the men, learned from Jim that Sorry was not back from Echo, and that Swan and Lone had gone down to the place where Frank had been found. She poured Jim's coffee and went on her tiptoes to see if her father still slept. She dreaded his awakening and the moment when she must tell him about Frank, and she had an unreasonable hope that the news might be kept from him until the doctor came again.

Brit was awake, and the look in his eyes frightened Lorraine so that she stopped in the middle of the room, staring at him fascinated.

"Well," he said flatly, "who is it this time? Lone, or - Frank?"

"Why - who is what?" Lorraine parried awkwardly. "I don't -"

"Did they git Frank, las' night?" Brit's eyes seemed to bore into her soul, searching pitilessly for the truth. "Don't lie to me, Raine - it ain't going to help any. Was it Frank or Lone? They's a dead man laid out on this ranch. Who is it?"

"F-frank," Lorraine stammered, backing away from him. "H-how did you know?"

"How did it happen?" Brit's eyes were terrible.

Lorraine shuddered while she told him.

"Rabbits in a trap," Brit muttered, staring at the low ceiling. "Can't prove nothing - couldn't convict anybody if we could prove it. Bill Warfield's got this county under his thumb. Rabbits in a trap. Raine, you better pack up and go home to your mother. There's goin' to be hell a-poppin' if I live to git outa this bed."

Lorraine stooped over him, and her eyes were almost as terrible as were Brit's. "Let it pop. We aren't quitters, are we, dad? I'm going to stay with you." Then she saw tears spilling over Brit's eyelids and left the room hurriedly, fighting back a storm of weeping. She herself could not mourn for Frank with any sense of great personal loss, but it was different with her dad. He and Frank had lived together for so many years that his loyal heart ached with grief for that surly, faithful old partner of his.

But Lorraine's fighting blood was up, and she could not waste time in weeping. She drank a cup of coffee, went out and called Jim, and told him that she was going to take a ride, and that she wanted a decent horse.

"You can take mine," Jim offered. "He's gentle and easy-gaited. I'll go saddle up. When do you want to go?"

"Right now, as soon as I'm ready. I'll fix dad's breakfast, and you can look after him until Lone and Swan come back. One of them will stay with him then. I may be gone for three or four hours. I'll go crazy if I stay here any longer."

Jim eyed her while he bit off a chew of tobacco. "It'd be a good thing if you had some neighbor woman come in and stay with yuh," he said slowly. "But there ain't any I can think of that'd be much force. You take Snake and ride around close and forget things for awhile." He hesitated, his hand moving slowly back to his pocket. "If yuh feel like you want a gun -"

Lorraine laughed bitterly. "You don't think any accident would happen to *me*, do you?"

"Well, no - e I wouldn't advise yuh to go ridin'," Jim said thoughtfully. "This here gun's kinda techy, anyway, unless you're used to a quick trigger. Yuh might be safer without it than with it."

By the time she was ready, Jim was tying his horse, Snake, to the corral. Lorraine walked slowly past the bunk-house with her face turned from it and her thoughts dwelling terrifiedly upon what lay within. Once she was past she began running, as if she were trying to outrun her thoughts. Jim watched her gravely, untied Snake and stood at his head while she mounted, then walked ahead of her to the gate and opened it for her.

"Yore nerves are sure shot to hell," he blurted sympathetically as she rode past him. "I guess you need a ride, all right. Snake's plumb safe, so yuh got no call to worry about him. Take it easy, Raine, on the worrying. That's about the worst thing you can do."

Lorraine gave him a grateful glance and a faint attempt at a smile, and rode up the trail she always took, - the trail where she had met Lone that day when he returned her purse, the trail that led to Fred Thurman's ranch and to Sugar Spring and, if you took a certain turn at a certain place, to Granite Ridge and beyond.

Up on the ridge nearest the house Al Woodruff shifted his position so that he could watch her go. He had been watching Lone and Swan and the dog, trailing certain tracks through the sagebrush down below, and when Lorraine rode away from the Quirt they were in the wagon road, fussing around the place where Frank had been found.

"They can't pin nothing on *me*," Al tried to comfort himself. "If that damn girl would keep her mouth shut I could stand a trial, even. They ain't got any evidence whatever, unless she saw me at Rock City that night." He turned and looked again toward the two men down on the road and tilted his mouth down at the corners in a sour grin.

"Go to it and be damned to you!" he muttered. "You haven't got the dope, and you can't git it, either. Trail that horse if you want to - I'd like to see yuh amuse yourselves that way!"

He turned again to stare after Lorraine, meditating deeply. If she had only been a man, he would have known exactly how to still her tongue, but he had never before been called upon to deal with the problem of keeping a woman quiet. He saw that she was taking the trail toward Fred Thurman's, and that she was riding swiftly, as if she had some errand in that direction, something urgent. Al was very adept at reading men's moods and intentions from small details in their behavior. He had seen Lorraine start on several leisurely, purposeless rides, and her changed manner held a significance which he did not attempt to belittle.

He led his horse down the side of the ridge opposite the road and the house, mounted there and rode away after Lorraine, keeping parallel with the trail but never using it, as was his habit. He made no attempt to overtake her, and not once did Lorraine glimpse him or suspect that she was being followed. Al knew well the art of concealing his movements and his proximity from the inquisitive eyes of another man's saddle horse, and Snake had no more suspicion than his rider that they were not altogether alone that morning.

Lorraine sent him over the trail at a pace which Jim had long since reserved for emergencies. But Snake appeared perfectly able and willing to hold it and never stumbled or slowed unexpectedly as did Yellowjacket, wherefore Lorraine rode faster than she would have done had she known more about horses.

Still, Snake held his own better than even Jim would have believed, and carried Lorraine up over Granite Ridge and down into the Sawtooth flat almost as quickly as Lorraine expected him to do. She came up to the Sawtooth ranch-houses with Snake in a lather of sweat and with her own determination unweakened to carry the war into the camp of her enemy. It was, she firmly believed, what should have been done long ago; what would have curbed effectually the arrogant powers of the Sawtooth.

She glanced at the foreman's cottage only to make sure that Hawkins was nowhere in sight there, and rode on toward the corrals, intercepting Hawkins and a large, well-groomed, smooth-faced man whom she knew at once must be Senator Warfield himself. Unconsciously Lorraine mentally fitted herself into a dramatic movie "scene" and plunged straight into the subject.

"There has been," she said tensely, "another Sawtooth accident. It worked better than the last one, when my father was sent over the grade into Spirit Canyon. Frank Johnson is *dead*. I am here to discover what you are going to do about it?" Her eyes were flashing, her chest was rising and falling rapidly when she had finished. She looked straight into Senator Warfield's face, her own full in the sunlight, so that, had there been a camera "shooting" the scene, her expression would have been fully revealed - though she did not realize all that.

Senator Warfield looked her over calmly (just as a director would have wished him to do) and turned to Hawkins. "Who is this girl?" he asked. "Is she the one who came here temporarily - deranged?"

"She's the girl," Hawkins affirmed, his eyes everywhere but on Lorraine's face. "Brit Hunter's daughter - they say."

"They *say*? I *am* his daughter! How dare you take that tone, Mr. Hawkins? My home is at the Quirt. When you strike at the Quirt you strike at me. When you strike at me I am going to strike back. Since I came here two men have been killed and my father has been nearly killed. He may die yet - I don't know what effect this shock will have upon him. But I know that Frank is dead, and that it's up to me now to see that justice is done. You - you cowards! You will kill a man for the sake of a few dollars, but you kill in the dark. You cover your murders under the pretense of accidents. I want to tell you this: Of all the men you have murdered, Frank Johnson will be avenged. You are going to answer for that. I shall see that you *do* answer for it! There is justice in this country, there *must* be. I'm going to demand that justice shall be measured out to you. I -"

"Was she violent, before?" Senator Warfield asked Hawkins in an undertone which Lorraine heard distinctly. "You're a deputy, Hawkins. If this keeps on, I'm afraid you will have to take her in and have her committed for insanity. It's a shame, poor thing. At her age it is pitiful. Look how she has ridden that horse! Another mile would have finished him."

"Do you mean to say you think I'm crazy? What an idea! It seems to me, Senator Warfield, that you are crazy yourself, to imagine that you can go on killing people and thinking you will never have to pay the penalty. You *will* pay. There is law in this land, even if -"

"This is pathetic," said Senator Warfield, still speaking to Hawkins. "Her father - if he is her father - is sick and not able to take care of her. We'll have to assume the responsibility ourselves, I'm afraid, Hawkins. She may harm herself, or -"

Lorraine turned white. She had never seen just such a situation arise in a screen story, but she knew what danger might lie in being accused of insanity. While Warfield was speaking, she had a swift vision of the evidence they could bring against her; how she had arrived there delirious after having walked out from Echo, - why, they would call even that a symptom of insanity! Lone had warned her of what people would say if she told any one of what she saw in Rock City, perhaps really believing that she had imagined it all. Lone might even think that she had some mental twist! Her world was reeling around her.

She whirled Snake on his hind feet, struck him sharply with the quirt and was galloping back over the trail past the Hawkins house before Senator Warfield had finished advising Hawkins. She saw Mrs. Hawkins standing in the door, staring at her, but she did not stop. They would take her to the asylum; she felt that the Sawtooth had the power, that she had played directly into their hands, and that they would be as ruthless in dealing with her as they had been with the nesters whom they had killed. She knew it, she had read it in the inscrutable, level look of Senator Warfield, in the half cringing, wholly subservient manner of Hawkins when he listened to his master.

"They're fiends!" she cried aloud once, while she urged Snake up the slope of Granite Ridge. "I believe they'd kill me if they were sure they could get away with it. But they could frame an insanity charge and put me - my God, what fiends they are!"

At the Sawtooth, Senator Warfield was talking with Mrs. Hawkins while her husband saddled two horses. Mrs. Hawkins lived within her four walls and called that, her "spere," and spoke of her husband as "he." You know the type of woman. That Senator Warfield was anything less than a godlike man who stood very high on the ladder of Fame, she would never believe. So she related garrulously certain incoherent, aimless utterances of Lorraine's, and cried a little, and thought it was perfectly awful that a sweet, pretty girl like that should be crazy. She would have made an ideal witness against Lorraine, her very sympathy carrying conviction of Lorraine's need of it. That she did not convince Senator Warfield of Lorraine's mental derangement was a mere detail. Senator Warfield had reasons for knowing that Lorraine was merely afflicted with a dangerous amount of knowledge and was using it without discretion.

"You mustn't let her run loose and maybe kill herself or somebody else!" Mrs. Hawkins exclaimed. "Oh, Senator, it's awful to think of! When she went past the house I knew the poor thing wasn't right -"

"We'll overtake her," Senator Warfield assured her comfortingly. "She can't go very far on that horse. She'd ridden him half to death, getting here. He won't hold out - he can't. She came here, I suppose, because she had been here before. A sanitarium may be able to restore her to a normal condition. I can't believe it's anything more than some nervous disorder. Now don't worry, my good woman. Just have a room ready, so that she will be comfortable here until we can get her to a sanitarium. It isn't hopeless, I assure you - but I'm mighty glad I happened to be here so that I can take charge of the case. Now here comes Hawkins. We'll bring her back - don't you worry."

"Well, take her away as quick as you can, Senator. I'm scared of crazy people. His brother went crazy in our house and -"

"Yes, yes - we'll take care of her. Poor girl, I wish that I had been here when she first came," said the senator, as he went to meet Hawkins, who was riding up from the corrals leading two horses - one for Lorraine, which shows what was his opinion of Snake.

## CHAPTER SEVENTEEN

## YACK DON'T LIE

For a time the trail seemed to lead toward Whisper. Then it turned away and seemed about to end abruptly on a flat outcropping of rock two miles from Whisper camp. Lone frowned and stared at the ground, and Swan spoke sharply to Jack, who was nosing back and forth, at fault if ever a dog was. But presently he took up the scent and led them down a barren slope and into grassy ground where a bunch of horses grazed contentedly. Jack singled out one and ran toward it silently, as he had done all his trailing that morning. The horse looked up, stared and went galloping down the little valley, stampeding the others with him.

"That's about where I thought we'd wind up - in a saddle bunch," Lone observed disgustedly. "If I had the evidence you're carrying in your pocket, Swan, I'd put that darn dog on the scent of the man, not the horse."

"The man I've got," Swan retorted. "I don't have to trail him."

"Well, now, you *think* you've got him. Here's good, level ground - I couldn't get outa sight in less than ten minutes, afoot. Let me walk out a ways, and you see if that handkerchief's mine. Oh, search me all you want to, first," he added, when he read the suspicion in Swan's eyes. "Make yourself safe as yuh please, but give me a fair show. You've made up your mind I'm the killer, and you've been fitting the evidence to me - or trying to."

"It fits," Swan pointed out drily.

"You see if it does. The dog'll tell you all about it in about two minutes if you give him a chance."

Swan looked at him. "Yack don't lie. By golly, I raised that dog to trail, and he *trails*, you bet! He's cocker spaniel and bloodhound, and he knows things, that dog. All right, Lone, you walk over to that black rock and set down. If you think you frame something, maybe, I pack a dead man to the Quirt again."

"You can, for all me," Lone replied quietly. "I'd about as soon go that way as the way I am now."

Swan watched him until he was seated on the rock as directed, his manacled hands resting on his knees, his face turned toward the horses. Then Swan took the blue handkerchief from his pocket, called Jack to him and muttered something in Swedish while the dog sniffed at the cloth. "Find him, Yack," said Swan, standing straight again.

Jack went sniffing obediently in wide circles, crossing unconcernedly Lone's footprints while he trotted back and forth. He hesitated once on the trail of the horse he had followed, stopped and looked at Swan inquiringly, and whined. Swan whistled the dog to him with a peculiar, birdlike note and called to Lone.

"You come back, Lone, and let Yack take a damn good smell of you. By golly, if that dog lies to me this time, I lick him good!"

Lone came back, grinning a little. "All right, now maybe you'll listen to reason. I ain't the kind to tell all I know and some besides, Swan. I've been a Sawtooth man, and a fellow kinda hates to throw down his outfit deliberate. But they're going too strong for any white man to stand for. I quit them when they tried to get Brit Hunter. I don't *know* so much, Swan, but I'm pretty good at guessing. So if you'll come with me to Whisper, your dog may show yuh who owns that handkerchief. If he don't, then I'm making a mistake, and I'd like to be set right."

"Somebody rode that horse," Swan meditated aloud. "Yack don't make a mistake like that, and I don't think I'm blind. Where's the man that was on the horse? What you think, Lone?"

"*Me*? I think there was another horse somewhere close to that outcropping, tied to a bush, maybe. I think the man you're after changed horses there, just on a chance that somebody might trail him from the road. You put your dog on the trail of that one particular horse, and he showed yuh where it was feeding with the bunch. It looks to me like it was turned loose, back there, and come on alone. Your man went to Whisper; I'll bank money on that. Anyway, your dog'll know if he's been there."

Swan thought it over, his eyes moving here and there to every hint of movement between the skyline and himself. Suddenly he turned to Lone, his face flushing with honest shame.

"Loney, take a damn Swede and give him something he believes, and you could pull his teeth before you pull that notion from his thick head. You acted funny, that day Fred Thurman was killed, and you gave yourself away at the stable when I showed you that saddle. So I think you're the killer, and I keep on thinking that, and I've been trying to catch you with evidence. I'm a Swede, all right! Square head. Built of wood two inches thick. Loney, you kick me good. You don't have time to ride over here, get some other horse and ride back to the Quirt after Frank was killed. You got there before I did, last night. We know Frank was dead not much more than one hour when we get him to the bunk-house. Yack, he gives you a good alibi."

"I sure am glad we took the time to trail that horse, then," Lone remarked, while Swan was removing the handcuffs. "You're all right, Swan. Nothing like sticking to an idea till you know it's wrong. Now, let's stick to mine for awhile. Let's go on to Whisper. It ain't far."

They returned to the rocky hillside where the trail had been covered, and searched here and there for the tracks of another horse; found the trail and followed it easily enough to Whisper.

Swan put Jack once more on the scent of the handkerchief, and if actions meant anything, Jack proved conclusively that he found the Whisper camp reeking with the scent.

But that was all, - since Al was at that moment trailing Lorraine toward the Sawtooth.

"We may as well eat," Swan suggested. "We'll get him, by golly, but we don't have to starve ourselves."

"He wouldn't know we're after him," Lone agreed. "He'll stick around so as not to raise suspicion. And he might come back, most any time. If he does, we'll say I'm out with you after coyotes, and we stopped here for a meal. That's good enough to satisfy him - till you get the drop on him. But I want to tell yuh, Swan, you can't take Al Woodruff as easy as you took me. And you couldn't have taken me so easy if I'd been the man you wanted. Al would kill you as easy as you kill coyotes. Give him a reason, and you won't need to give him a chance along with it. He'll find the chance himself."

Because they thought it likely that Al would soon return, they did not hurry. They were hungry, and they cooked enough food for four men and ate it leisurely. Jim was at the ranch, Sorry had undoubtedly returned before now, and the coroner would probably not arrive before noon, at the earliest.

Swan wanted to take Al Woodruff back with him in irons. He wanted to confront the coroner with the evidence he had found and the testimony which Lone could give. There had been too many killings already, he asserted in his naive way; the sooner Al Woodruff was locked up, the safer the country would be.

He discussed with Lone the possibility of making Al talk, - the chance of his implicating the Sawtooth. Lone did not hope for much and said so.

"If Al was a talker he wouldn't be holding the job he's got," Lone argued. "Don't get the wrong idea again, Swan. Yuh may pin this on to Al, but that won't let the Sawtooth in. The Sawtooth's too slick for that. They'd be more likely to make up a lynching party right in the outfit and hang Al as an example than they would try to shield him. He's played a lone hand, Swan, right from the start, unless I'm badly mistaken. The Sawtooth's paid him for playing it, that's all."

"Warfield, he's the man I want," Swan confided. "It's for more than killing these men. It goes into politics, Loney, and it goes deep. He's bad for the government. Getting Warfield for having men killed is getting Warfield without telling secrets of politics. Warfield, he's a smart man, by golly. He knows some one is after him in politics, but he don't know some one is after him at home. So the big Swede has got to be smart enough to get the evidence against him for killing."

"Well, I wish yuh luck, Swan, but I can't say you're going at it right. Al won't talk, I tell yuh."

Swan did not believe that. He waited another hour and made a mental inventory of everything in camp while he waited. Then, chiefly because Lone's impatience finally influenced him, he set out to see where Al had gone.

According to Jack, Al had gone to the corral. From there they put Jack on the freshest hoofprints leaving the place, and were led here and there in an apparently aimless journey to nowhere until, after Jack had been at fault in another rock patch, the trail took them straight away to the ridge overlooking the Quirt ranch. The two men looked at one another.

"That's like Al," Lone commented drily. "Coyotes are foolish, alongside him, and you'll find it out. I'll bet he's been watching this place since daybreak."

"Where he goes, Yack will follow," Swan grinned cheerfully. "And I follow Yack. We'll get him, Lone. That dog, he never quits till I say quit."

"You better go down and get a horse, then," Lone advised. "They're all gentle. Al's mounted, remember. He's maybe gone over to the Sawtooth, and that's farther than you can walk."

"I can walk all day and all night, when I need to go like that. I can take short cuts that a horse can't take. I think I shall go on my own legs."

"Well, I'm going down to the house first. I know them two men riding down to the gate. I want to see what the boss and Hawkins have got to say about this last 'accident.' Better come on down, Swan. You might pick up something. They're heading for the ranch, all right. Going to make a play at being neighborly, I reckon."

"You bet I want to see Warfield," Swan assented rather eagerly and called Jack, who had nosed around the spot where Al had waited so long and was now trotting along the ridge on the next lap of Al's journey.

They reached the gate in time to meet Warfield and Hawkins face to face. Hawkins gave Lone a quick, questioning look and nodded carelessly to Swan. Warfield, having a delicate errand to perform and knowing how much depended upon first impressions, pulled up eagerly when he recognized Lone.

"Has the girl arrived safely, Lone?" he asked anxiously.

"What girl?" Lone looked at him noncommittally.

"Miss - ah - Hunter. Have you been away all the forenoon? The girl came to the ranch in such a condition that I was afraid she might do herself or some one else an injury. Has she been unbalanced for long?"

"If you mean Lorraine Hunter, she was all right last time I saw her, and that was last night." Lone's eyes narrowed a little as he watched the two. "You say she went to the Sawtooth?"

"She came pelting over there crazier than when you brought her in," Hawkins broke in gruffly. "She ain't safe going around alone like that."

Senator Warfield glanced at him impatiently. "Is there any truth in her declaring that Frank Johnson is dead? She seemed to have had a shock of some kind. She was raving crazy, and in her rambling talk she said something about Frank Johnson having died last night."

Lone glanced back as he led the way through the gate which Swan was holding open. "He didn't die - he got killed last night," he corrected.

"Killed! And how did that happen? It was impossible to get two coherent sentences out of the girl." Senator Warfield rode through just behind Lone and reined close, lowering his voice. "No use in letting this get out," he said confidentially. "It may be that the girl's dementia is some curable nervous disorder, and you know what an injustice it would be if it became noised around that the girl is crazy. How much English does that Swede know?"

"Not any more than he needs to get along on," Lone answered, instinctively on guard. "He's all right - just a good-natured kinda cuss that wouldn't harm anybody."

He glanced uneasily at the house, hoping that Lorraine was safe inside, yet fearing that she would not be safe anywhere. Sane or insane, she was in danger if Senator Warfield considered her of sufficient importance to bring him out on horseback to the Quirt ranch. Lone knew how seldom the owner of the Sawtooth rode on horseback since he had high-powered cars to carry him in soft comfort.

"I'll go see if she's home," Lone explained, and reined John Doe toward the house.

"I'll go with you," Senator Warfield offered suavely and kept alongside. "Frank Johnson was killed, you say? How did it happen?"

"Fell off his wagon and broke his neck," Lone told him laconically. "Brit's pretty sick yet; I don't guess you'd better go inside. There's been a lot of excitement already for the old man. He only sees folks he's used to having around."

With that he dismounted and went into the house, leaving Senator Warfield without an excuse for following. Swan and Hawkins came up and waited with him, and Jim opened the door of the bunk-house and looked out at them without showing enough interest to come forward and speak to them.

In a few minutes Lone returned, to find Senator Warfield trying to glean information from Swan, who seemed willing enough to give it if only he could find enough English words to form a complete sentence. Swan, then, had availed himself of Lone's belittlement of him and was living down to it. But Lone gave him scant attention just then.

"She hasn't come back. Brit's worked himself up into a fever, and I didn't dare tell him she wasn't with me. I said she's all tired out and sick and wanted to stay up by the spring awhile, where it's cool. I said she was with me, and the sun was too much for her, and she sent him word that Jim would take care of him awhile longer. So you better move down this way, or he'll hear us talking and want to know what's up."

"You're sure she isn't here?" Senator Warfield's voice held suspicion.

"You can ask Jim, over here. He's been on hand right along. And if you can't take his word for it, you can go look in the shack - but in that case Brit's liable to take a shot at yuh, Senator. He's on the warpath right, and he's got his gun right handy."

"It is not necessary to search the cabin," Senator Warfield answered stiffly. "Unless she is in a stupor we'd have heard her yelling long ago. The girl was a raving maniac when she appeared at the Sawtooth. It's for her good that I'm thinking."

Jim stepped out of the doorway and came slowly toward them, eyeing the two from the Sawtooth curiously while he chewed tobacco. His hands rested on his hips, his thumbs hooked inside his overalls; a gawky pose that fitted well his colorless personality, - and left his right hand close to his six-shooter.

"Cor'ner comin'?" he asked, nodding at the two who were almost strangers to him. "Sorry, he got back two hours ago, and he said the cor'ner would be right out. But he ain't showed up yet."

Senator Warfield said that he felt sure the coroner would be prompt and then questioned Jim artfully about "Miss Hunter."

"Raine? She went fer a ride. I loaned her my horse, and she ain't back yet. I told her to take a good long ride and settle her nerves. She acted kinda edgy."

Senator Warfield and his foreman exchanged glances for which Lone could have killed them.

"You noticed, then, that she was not quite - herself?" Senator Warfield used his friendly, confidential tone on Jim.

"We-ell - yes, I did. I thought a ride would do her good, mebby. She's been sticking here on the job purty close. And Frank getting killed kinda - upset her, I guess."

"That's it - that's what I was saying. Disordered nerves, which rest and proper medical care will soon remedy." He looked at Lone. "Her horse was worn out when she reached the ranch. Does she know this country well? She started this way, and she should have been here some time ago. We thought it best to ride after her, but there was some delay in getting started. Hawkins' horse broke away and gave us some trouble catching him, so the girl had quite a start. But with her horse fagged as it was, we had no idea that we would fail to get even a sight of her. She may have wandered off on some other trail, in which case her life as well as her reason is in danger."

Lone did not answer at once. It had occurred to him that Senator Warfield knew where Lorraine was at that minute, and that he might be showing this concern for the effect it would have on his hearers. He looked at him speculatively.

"Do you think we ought to get out and hunt for her?" he asked.

"I certainly think some one ought to. We can't let her wander around the country in that condition. If she is not here, she is somewhere in the hills, and she should be found."

"She sure ain't here," Jim asserted convincingly. "I been watching for the last two hours, expecting every minute she'd show up. I'd a been kinda oneasy, myself, but Snake's dead gentle, and she's a purty fair rider fer a girl."

"Then we'll have to find her. Lone, can you come and help?"

"The Swede and me'll both help," Lone volunteered. "Jim and Sorry can wait here for the coroner. We ought to find her without any trouble, much. Swan, I'll get you that tobacco first and see if Brit needs anything."

He started to the house, and Swan followed him aimlessly, his long strides bringing him close to Lone before they reached the door.

"What do you make of this new play?" Lone muttered cautiously when he saw Swan's shadow move close to his own.

"By golly, it's something funny about it. You stick with them, Loney, and find out. I'm taking Al's trail with Yack. You fix it." And he added whimsically, "Not so much tobacco, Lone. I don't eat it or smoke it ever in my life."

His voice was very Swedish, which was fortunate, because Senator Warfield appeared softly behind him and went into the house.

Swan was startled, but he hadn't much time to worry over the possibility of having been overheard. Brit's voice rose in a furious denunciation of Bill Warfield, punctuated by two shots and followed almost immediately by the senator.

"My God, the whole family's crazy!" Warfield exclaimed, when he had reached the safety of the open air. "You're right, Lone. I thought I'd be neighborly enough to ask what I could do for him, and he tried to kill me!"

Lone merely grunted and gave Swan the tobacco.

## CHAPTER EIGHTEEN

## "I THINK AL WOODRUFF'S GOT HER"

There was no opportunity for further conference. Senator Warfield showed no especial interest in Swan, and the Swede was permitted without comment to take his dog and strike off up the ridge. Jim and Sorry were sent to look after Brit, who was still shouting vain threats against the Sawtooth, and the three men rode away together. Warfield did not suggest separating, though Lone expected him to do so, since one man on a trail was as good as three in a search of this kind.

He was still inclined to doubt the whole story. He did not believe that Lorraine had been to the Sawtooth, or that she had raved about anything. She had probably gone off by herself to cry and to worry over her troubles, - hurt, too, perhaps, because Lone had left the ranch that morning without a word with her first. He believed the story of her being insane had been carefully planned, and that Warfield had perhaps ridden over in the hope that they would find her alone; though with Frank dead on the ranch that would be unlikely. But to offset that, Lone's reason told him that Warfield had probably not known that Frank was dead. That had been news to him - or had it? He tried to remember whether Warfield had mentioned it first and could not. Too many disturbing emotions had held him lately; Lone was beginning to feel the need of a long, quiet pondering over his problems. He did not feel sure of anything except the fact that the Quirt was like a drowning man struggling vainly against the whirlpool that is sucking him slowly under.

One thing he knew, and that was his determination to stay with these two of the Sawtooth until he had some definite information; until he saw Lorraine or knew that she was safe from them. Like a weight pressing harder and harder until one is crushed beneath it, their talk of Lorraine's insanity forced fear into his soul. They could do just what they had talked of doing. He himself had placed that weapon in their hands when he took her to the Sawtooth delirious and told of wilder words and actions. Hawkins and his wife would swear away her sanity if they were told to do it, and there were witnesses in plenty who had heard him call her crazy that first morning.

They could do it; they could have her committed to an asylum, or at least to a sanitarium. He did not underestimate the influence of Senator Warfield. And what could the Quirt do to prevent the outrage? Frank Johnson was dead; Brit was out of the fight for the time being; Jim and Sorry were the doggedly faithful sort who must have a leader before they can be counted upon to do much.

Swan, - Lone lifted his head and glanced toward the ridge when he thought of Swan. There, indeed, he might hope for help. But Swan was out here, away from reinforcements. He was trailing Al Woodruff, and when he found him, - that might be the end of Swan. If not, Warfield could hurry Lorraine away before Swan could act in the matter. A whimsical thought of Swan's telepathic miracle crossed his mind and was dismissed as an unseemly bit of foolery in a matter so grave as Lorraine's safety. And yet - the doctor *had* received a message that he was wanted at the Quirt, and he had arrived before his patient. There was no getting around that, however impossible it might be. No one could have foreseen Brit's accident; no one save the man who had prepared it for him, and he would be the last person to call for help.

"We followed the girl's horse-tracks almost to Thurman's place and lost the trail there." Warfield turned in the saddle to look at Lone riding behind him. "We made no particular effort to trace her from there, because we were sure she would come on home. I'm going back that far, and we'll pick up the trail, unless we find her at the ranch. She may have hidden herself away. You can't," he added, "be sure of anything where a demented person is concerned. They never act according to logic or reason, and it is impossible to make any deductions as to their probable movements."

Lone nodded, not daring to trust his tongue with speech just then. If he were to protect Lorraine later on, he knew that he must not defend her now.

"Hawkins told me she had some sort of hallucination that she had seen a man killed at Rock City, when she was wandering around in that storm," Warfield went on in a careless, gossipy tone. "Just what was that about, Lone? You're the one who found her and took her in to the ranch, I believe. She somehow mixed her delusion up with Fred Thurman, didn't she?"

Lone made a swift decision. He was afraid to appear to hesitate, so he laughed his quiet little chuckle while he scrambled mentally for a plausible lie.

"I don't know as she done that, quite," he drawled humorously. "She was out of her head, all right, and talking wild, but I laid it to her being sick and scared. She said a man was shot, and that she saw it happen. And right on top of that she said she didn't think they ought to stage a murder and a thunderstorm in the same scene, and thought they ought to save the thunder and lightning for the murderer to make his getaway by. She used to work for the moving pictures, and she was going on about some wild-west picture she thought she was acting a part in.

"Afterwards I told her what she'd been saying, and she seemed to kinda remember it, like a bad dream she'd had. She told me she thought the villain in one of the plays she acted in had pulled off a stage murder in them rocks. We figured it out together that the first crack of thunder had sounded like shooting, and that's what started her off. She hadn't ever been in a real thunderstorm before, and she's scared of them. I know that one we had the other day like to of scared her into hysterics. I laughed at her and joshed her out of it."

"Didn't she ever say anything about Fred Thurman, then?" Warfield persisted.

"Not to me, she didn't. Fred was dragged that night, and if she heard about a man being killed during that same storm, she might have said something about it. She might have wondered if that was what she saw. I don't know. She's pretty sensible - when she ain't crazy."

Warfield turned his horse, as if by accident, so that he was brought face to face with Lone. His eyes searched Lone's face pitilessly.

"Lone, you know how ugly a story can grow if it's left alone. Do *you* believe that girl actually saw a man shot? Or do you think she was crazy?"

Lone met Warfield's eyes fairly. "I think she was plumb out of her head," he answered. And he added with just the right degree of hesitation: "I don't think she's what you'd call right crazy, Mr. Warfield. Lots of folks go outa their heads and talk crazy when they get a touch of fever, and they get over it again."

"Let's have a fair understanding," Warfield insisted. "Do you think I am justified in the course I am taking, or don't you?"

"Hunting her up? Sure, I do! If you and Hawkins rode on home, I'd keep on hunting till I located her. If she's been raving around like you say, she's in no shape to be riding these hills alone. She's got to be taken care of."

Warfield gave him another sharp scrutiny and rode on. "I always prefer to deal in the open with every one," he averred. "It may not be my affair, strictly speaking. The Quirt and the Sawtooth aren't very intimate. But the Quirt's having trouble enough to warrant any one in lending a hand; and common humanity demands that I take charge of the girl until she is herself again."

"I don't know as any one would question that," Lone assented and ground his teeth afterwards because he must yield even the appearance of approval. He knew that Warfield must feel himself in rather a desperate position, else he would never trouble to make his motives so clear to one of his men. Indeed, Warfield had protested his unselfishness in the matter too much and too often to have deceived the dullest man who owned the slightest suspicion of him. Lone could have smiled at the sight of Senator Warfield betraying himself so, had smiling been possible to him then.

He dropped behind the two at the first rough bit of trail and felt stealthily to test the hanging of his six-shooter, which he might need in a hurry. Those two men would never lay their hands on Lorraine Hunter while he lived to prevent it. He did not swear it to himself; he had no need.

They rode on to Fred Thurman's ranch, dismounted at Warfield's suggestion - which amounted to a command - and began a careful search of the premises. If Warfield had felt any doubt of Lone's loyalty he appeared to have dismissed it from his mind, for he sent Lone to the stable to search there, while he and Hawkins went into the house. Lone guessed that the two felt the need of a private conference after their visit to the Quirt, but he could see no way to slip unobserved to the house and eavesdrop, so he looked perfunctorily through all the sheds and around the depleted haystacks, - wherever a person could find a hiding place. He was letting himself down through the manhole in the stable loft when Swan's voice, lowered almost to a whisper, startled him.

"What the hell!" Lone ejaculated under his breath. "I thought you were on another trail!"

"That trail leads here, Lone. Did you find Raine yet?"

"Not a sign of her. Swan, I don't know what to make of it. I did think them two were stalling. I thought they either hadn't seen her at all, or had got hold of her and were trying to square themselves on the insanity dodge. But if they know where she is, they're acting damn queer, Swan. They *want* her. They haven't got her yet."

"They're in the house," Swan reassured Lone. "I heard them walking. You don't think they've got her there, Lone?"

"If they have," gritted Lone, "they made the biggest blunder of their lives bringing me over here. No, I could see they wanted to get off alone and hold a powwow. They expected she'd be at the Quirt."

"I think Al Woodruff, he's maybe got her, then," Swan declared, after studying the matter briefly. "All the way he follows the trail over here, Lone. I could see you sometimes in the trail. He was keeping hid from the trail - I think because Raine was riding along, this morning, and he's following. The tracks are that old."

"They said they had trailed Raine this far, coming from the Sawtooth," Lone told him worriedly. "What do you think Al would want -"

"Don't she see him shoot Fred Thurman? By golly, I'm scared for that girl, Loney!"

Lone stared at him. "He wouldn't dare!"

"A coward is a brave man when you scare him bad enough," Swan stated flatly. "I'm careful always when I corner a coward."

"Al ain't a coward. You've got him wrong."

"Maybe, but he kills like a coward would kill, and he's scared he will be caught. Warfield, he's scared, too. You watch him, Lone.

"Now I tell you what I do. Yack, he picks up the trail from here to where you can follow easy. We know two places where he didn't go with her, and from here is two more trails he could take. But one goes to the main road, and he don't take that one, I bet you. I think he takes that girl up Spirit Canyon, maybe. It's woods and wild country in a few miles, and plenty of places to hide, and good chances for getting out over the top of the divide.

"I'm going to my cabin, and you don't say anything when I leave. Warfield, he don't want the damn Swede hanging around. So you go with them, Loney. This is to what you call a show-down."

"We'll want the dog," Lone told him, but Swan shook his head. Hawkins and Warfield had come from the house and were approaching the stable. Swan looked at Lone, and Lone went forward to meet them.

"The Swede followed along on the ridge, and he didn't see anything," he volunteered, before Warfield could question him. "We might put his dog on the trail and see which way she went from here."

Warfield thought that a good idea. He was so sure that Lorraine must be somewhere within a mile or two of the place that he seemed to think the search was practically over when Jack, nosing out the trail of Al Woodruff, went trotting toward Spirit Canyon.

"Took the wrong turn after she left the corrals here," Warfield commented relievedly. "She wouldn't get far, up this way."

"There's the track of two horses," Hawkins said abruptly. "That there is the girl's horse, all right - there's a hind shoe missing. We saw where her horse had cast a shoe, coming over Juniper Ridge. But there's another horse track.'

Lone bit his lip. It was the other horse that Jack had been trailing so long. "There was a loose horse hanging around Thurman's place," he said casually. "It's him, tagging along, I reckon."

"Oh," said Hawkins. "That accounts for it."

## CHAPTER NINETEEN

## SWAN CALLS FOR HELP

Past the field where the horses were grazing and up the canyon on the side toward Skyline Meadow, that lay on a shoulder of Bear Top, the dog nosed unfalteringly along the trail. Now and then he was balked when the hoofprints led him to the bank of Granite Creek, but not for long. Jack appeared to understand why his trailing was interrupted and sniffed the bank until he picked up the scent again.

"Wonder if she changed off and rode that loose horse," Hawkins said once, when the tracks were plain in the soft soil of the creek bank. "She might, and lead that horse she was on."

"She wouldn't know enough. She's a city girl," Lone replied, his heart heavy with fear for Lorraine.

"Well, she ain't far off then," Hawkins comforted himself. "Her horse acted about played out when she hit the ranch. She had him wet from his ears to his tail, and he was breathin' like that Ford at the ranch. If that's a sample of her riding, she ain't far off."

"Crazy - to ride up here. Keep your eyes open, boys. We must find her, whatever we do." Warfield gazed apprehensively at the rugged steeps on either hand and at the timber line above them. "From here on she couldn't turn back without meeting us - if I remember this country correctly. Could she, Hawkins?"

"Not unless she turned off, up here a mile or two, into that gulch that heads into Skyline," said Hawkins. "There's a stock trail part way down from the top where it swings off from the divide to Wilder Creek."

Swan, walking just behind Hawkins, moved up a pace.

"I could go on Skyline with Yack, and I could come down by those trail," he suggested diffidently, Swedishly, yet with a certain compelling confidence. "What you think?"

"I think that's a damned good idea for a square head," Hawkins told him, and repeated it to Warfield, who was riding ahead.

"Why, yes. We don't need the dog, or the man either. Go up to the head of the gulch and keep your eyes open, Swan. We'll meet you up here. You know the girl, don't you?"

"Yas, Ay know her pretty good," grinned Swan.

"Well, don't frighten her. Don't let her see that you think anything is wrong - and don't say anything about us. We made the mistake of discussing her condition within her hearing, and it is possible that she understood enough of what we were saying to take alarm. You understand? Don't tell girl she's crazy." He tapped his head to make his meaning plainer. "Don't tell girl we're looking for her. You understand?"

"Yas, Ay know English pretty good. Ay don't tell too moch." His cheerful smile brought a faint response from Senator Warfield. At Lone he did not look at all. "I go quick. I'm good climber like a sheep," he boasted, and whistling to Jack, he began working his way up a rough, brush-scattered ledge to the slope above.

Lone watched him miserably, wishing that Swan was not quite so matter of fact in his man-chasing. If Al Woodruff, for some reason which Lone could not fathom, had taken Lorraine and forced her to go with him into the wilderness, Warfield and Hawkins would be his allies the moment they came up with him.

Lone was no coward, but neither was he a fool. Hawkins had never distinguished himself as a fighter, but Lone had gleaned here and there a great deal of information about Senator Warfield in the old days when he had been plain Bill. When Lorraine and Al were overtaken, then Lone would need to show the stuff that was in him. He only hoped he would have time, and that luck would be with him.

"If they get me, it'll be all off with her," he worried, as he followed the two up the canyon. "Swan would have been a help. But he thinks more of catching Al than he does of helping Raine."

He looked up and saw that already Swan was halfway up the canyon's steep side, making his way through the brush with more speed than Lone could have shown on foot in the open, unless he ran. The sight heartened Lone a little. Swan might have some plan of his own, - an ambush, possibly. If he would only keep along within rifle shot and remain hidden, he would show real brains, Lone thought. But Swan, when Lone looked up again, was climbing straight away from the little searching party; and even though he seemed tireless on foot, he could not perform miracles.

Swan, however, was not troubling himself over what Lone would think, or even what Warfield was thinking. Contrary to Lone's idea of him, Swan was tired, and he was thinking a great deal about Lorraine, and very little about Al Woodruff, except as Al was concerned with Lorraine's welfare. Swan had made a mistake, and he was humiliated over his blunder. Al had kept himself so successfully in the background while Lone's peculiar actions had held his attention, that Swan had never considered Al Woodruff as the killer. Now he blamed himself for Frank's death. He had been watching Lone, had been baffled by Lone's consistent kindness toward the Quirt, by the force of his personality which held none of the elements of cold-blooded murder. He had believed that he had the Sawtooth killer under observation, and he had been watching and waiting for evidence that would impress a grand jury. And all the while he had let Al Woodruff ride free and unsuspected.

The one stupid thing, in Swan's opinion, which he had not done was to let Lone go on holding his tongue. He had forced the issue that morning. He had wanted to make Lone talk, had hoped for a weakening and a confession. Instead he had learned a good deal which he should have known before.

As he forged up the slope across the ridged lip of the canyon, his one immediate object was speed. Up the canyon and over the divide on the west shoulder of Bear Top was a trail to the open country beyond. It was perfectly passable, as Swan knew; he had packed in by that trail when he located his homestead on Bear Top. That is why he had his cabin up and was living in it before the Sawtooth discovered his presence.

Al, he believed, was making for Bear Top Pass. Once down the other side he would find friends to lend him fresh horses. Swan had learned something of these friends of the Sawtooth, and he could guess pretty accurately how far some of them would go in their service. Fresh horses for Al, food - perhaps even a cabin where he could hide Lorraine away - were to be expected from any one of them, once Al was over the divide.

Swan glanced up at the sun, saw that it was dropping to late afternoon and started in at a long, loose-jointed trot across the mountain meadow called Skyline. A few pines, with scattered clumps of juniper and fir, dotted the long, irregular stretch of grassland which formed the meadow. Range cattle were feeding here and there, so wild they lifted heads to stare at the man and dog, then came trotting forward, their curiosity unabated by the fact that they had seen these two before.

Jack looked up at his master, looked at the cattle and took his place at Swan's heels. Swan shouted and flung his arms, and the cattle ducked, turned and galloped awkwardly away. Swan's trot did not slacken. His rifle swung rhythmically in his right hand, the muzzle tilted downward. Beads of perspiration on his forehead had merged into tiny rivulets on his cheeks and dripped off his clean-lined, square jaw. Still he ran, his breath unlabored yet coming in whispery aspirations from his great lungs.

The full length of Skyline Meadow he ran, jumping the small beginning of Wilder Creek with one great leap that scarcely interrupted the beautiful rhythm of his stride. At the far end of the clearing, snuggled between two great pines that reached high into the blue, his squatty cabin showed red-brown against the precipitous shoulder of Bear Top peak, covered thick with brush and scraggy timber whipped incessantly by the wind that blew over the mountain's crest.

At the door Swan stopped and examined the crude fastening of the door; made himself certain, by private marks of his own, that none had entered in his absence, and went in with a great sigh of satisfaction. It was still broad daylight, though the sun's rays slanted in through the window; but Swan lighted a lantern that hung on a nail behind the door, carried it across the neat little room, and set it down on the floor beside the usual pioneer cupboard made simply of clean boxes nailed bottom against the wall. Swan had furnished a few extra frills to his cupboard, for the ends of the boxes were fastened to hewn slabs standing upright and just clearing the floor. Near the upper shelf a row of nails held Swan's coffee cups, - four of them, thick and white, such as cheap restaurants use.

Swan hooked a finger over the nail that held a cracked cup and glanced over his shoulder at Jack, sitting in the doorway with his keen nose to the world.

"You watch out now, Yack. I shall talk to my mother with my thoughts," he said, drawing a hand across his forehead and speaking in breathless gasps. "You watch."

For answer Jack thumped his tail on the dirt floor and sniffed the breeze, taking in his overlapping tongue while he did so. He licked his lips, looked over his shoulder at Swan, and draped his pink tongue down over his lower jaw again.

"All right, now I talk," said Swan and pulled upon the nail in his fingers.

The cupboard swung toward him bodily, end slabs and all. He picked up the lantern, stepped over the log sill and pulled the cupboard door into place again.

Inside the dugout Swan set the lantern on a table, dropped wearily upon a rough bench before it and looked at the jars beside him, lifted his hand and opened a compact, but thoroughly efficient field wireless "set." His right fingers dropped to the key, and the whining drone of the wireless rose higher and higher as he tuned up. He reached for his receivers, ducked his head and adjusted them with one hand, and sent a call spitting tiny blue sparks from the key under his fingers.

He waited, repeating the call. His blue eyes clouded with anxiety and he fumbled the adjustments, coaxing the current into perfect action before he called again. Answer came, and Swan bent over the table, listening, his eyes fixed vacantly upon the opposite wall of the dugout. Then, his fingers flexing delicately, swiftly, he sent the message that told how completely his big heart matched the big body:

> "Send doctor and trained nurse to Quirt ranch at once. Send men to Bear Top Pass, intercept man with young woman, or come to rescue if he don't cross. Have three men here with evidence to convict if we can save the girl who is valuable witness. Girl being abducted in fear of what she can tell. They plan to charge her with insanity. Urgent. Hurry. Come ready to fight.
>
> "S.V."

Swan had a code, but codes require a little time in the composition of a message, and time was the one thing he could not waste. He heard the gist of the message repeated to him, told the man at the other station that lives were at stake, and threw off the current.

## CHAPTER TWENTY

## KIDNAPPED

Lorraine had once had a nasty fall from riding down hill at a gallop. She remembered that accident and permitted Snake to descend Granite Ridge at a walk, which was fortunate, since it gave the horse a chance to recover a little from the strain of the terrific pace at which she had ridden him that morning. At first it had been fighting fury that had impelled her to hurry; now it was fear that drove her homeward where Lone was, and Swan, and that stolid, faithful Jim. She felt that Senator Warfield would never dare to carry out his covert threat, once she reached home. Nevertheless, the threat haunted her, made her glance often over her shoulder.

At the Thurman ranch, which she was passing with a sickening memory of the night when she and Swan had carried her father there, Al Woodruff rode out suddenly from behind the stable and blocked the trail, his six-shooter in his hand, his face stony with determination. Lorraine afterwards decided that he must have seen or heard her coming down the ridge and had waited for her there. He smiled with his lips when she pulled up Snake with a startled look.

"You're in such a hurry this morning that I thought the only way to get a chance to talk to you was to hold you up," he said, in much the same tone he had used that day at the ranch.

"I don't see why you want to talk to me," Lorraine retorted, not in the least frightened at the gun, which was too much like her movie West to impress her much. But her eyes widened at the look in his face, and she tried to edge away from him without seeming to do so.

Al stopped her by the simple method of reaching out his left hand and catching Snake by the cheek-piece of the bridle. "You don't have to see why," he said. "I've been thinking a lot about you lately. I've made up my mind that I've got to have you with me - always. This is kinda sudden, maybe, but that's the way the game runs, sometimes. Now, I want to tell yuh one or two things that's for your own good. One is that I'll have my way, or die getting it. Don't be scared; I won't hurt you. But if you try to break away, I'll shoot you, that's all. I'm going to marry you, see, first. Then I'll make love to you afterwards. I ain't asking you if you'll marry me. You're going to do it, or I'll kill you."

Lorraine gazed at him fascinated, too astonished to attempt any move toward escape. Al's hand slipped from the bridle down to the reins, and still holding Snake, still holding the gun muzzle toward her, still looking her straight in the eyes, he threw his right leg over the cantle of his saddle and stepped off his horse.

"Put your other hand on the saddle horn," he directed. "I ain't going to hurt you if you're good."

He twitched his neckerchief off - Lorraine saw that it was untied, and that he must have planned all this - and with it he tied her wrists to the saddle horn. She gave Snake a kick in the ribs, but Al checked the horse's first start and Snake was too tired to dispute a command to stand still. Al put up his gun, pulled a hunting knife from a little scabbard in his boot, sliced two pairs of saddle strings from Lorraine's saddle, calmly caught and held her foot when she tried to kick him, pushed the foot back into the stirrup and tied it there with one of the leather strings. Just as if he were engaged in an everyday proceeding, he walked around Snake and tied Lorraine's right foot; then, to prevent her from foolishly throwing herself from the horse and getting hurt, he tied the stirrups together under the horse's belly.

"Now, if you'll be a good girl, I'll untie your hands," he said, glancing up into her face. He freed her hands, and Lorraine immediately slapped him in the face and reached for his gun. But Al was too quick for her. He stepped back, picked up Snake's reins and mounted his own horse. He looked back at her appraisingly, saw her glare of hatred and grinned at it, while he touched his horse with the spurs and rode away, leading Snake behind him.

Lorraine said nothing until Al, riding at a lope, passed the field at the mouth of Spirit Canyon where the blaze-faced roan still fed with the others. They were feeding along the creek quite close to the fence, and the roan walked toward them. The sight of it stirred Lorraine out of her dumb horror.

"You killed Fred Thurman! I saw you," she cried suddenly.

"Well, you ain't going to holler it all over the country," Al flung back at her over his shoulder. "When you're married to me, you'll come mighty close to keeping your mouth shut about it."

"I'll never marry you! You - you fiend! Do you think I'd marry a cold-blooded murderer like you?"

Al turned in the saddle and looked at her intently. "If I'm all that," he told her coolly, "you can figure out about what'll happen to you if you *don't* marry me. If you saw what I done to Fred Thurman, what do you reckon I'd do to *you*?" He looked at her for a minute, shrugged his shoulders and rode on, crossing the creek and taking a trail which Lorraine did not know. Much of the time they traveled in the water, though it slowed their pace. Where the trail was rocky, they took it and made better time.

Snake lagged a little on the upgrades, but he was well trained to lead and gave little trouble. Lorraine thought longingly of Yellowjacket and his stubbornness and tried to devise some way of escape. She could not believe that fate would permit Al Woodruff to carry out such a plan. Lone would overtake them, perhaps, - and then she remembered that Lone would have no means of knowing which way she had gone. If Hawkins and Senator Warfield came after them, her plight would be worse than ever. Still, she decided that she must risk that danger and give Lone a clue.

She dropped a glove beside the trail, where it lay in plain sight of any one following them. But presently Al looked over his shoulder, saw that one of her hands was bare, and tied Snake's reins to his saddle and his own horse to a bush. Then he went back down the trail until he found the glove. He put it into his pocket, came silently up to Lorraine and pulled off her other glove. Without a word he took her wrists in a firm clasp, tied them together again to the saddle horn, pulled off her tie, her hat, and the pins from her hair.

"I guess you don't know me yet," he remarked dryly, when he had confiscated every small article which she could let fall as she rode. "I was trying to treat yuh white, but you don't seem to appreciate it. Now you can ride hobbled, young lady."

"Oh, I could *kill* you!" Lorraine whispered between set teeth.

"You mean you'd like to. Well, I ain't going to give you a chance." His eyes rested on her face with a new expression; an awakening desire for her, an admiration for the spirit that would not let her weep and plead with him.

"Say! you ain't going to be a bit hard to marry," he observed, his eyes lighting with what was probably his nearest approach to tenderness. "I kinda wish you liked me, now I've got you."

He shook her arm and laughed when she turned her face away from him, then remounted his horse. Snake moved reluctantly when Al started on. Lorraine felt hope slipping from her. With her hands tied, she could do nothing at all save sit there and ride wherever Al Woodruff chose to lead her horse. He seemed to be making for the head of Spirit Canyon, on the side toward Bear Top.

As they climbed higher, she could catch glimpses of the road down which her father had driven almost to his death. She studied Al's back as he rode before her and wondered if he could really be cold-blooded enough to kill without compunction whoever he was told to kill, whether he had any personal quarrel with his victim or not. Certainly he had had no quarrel with her father, or with Frank.

It was long past noon, and she was terribly hungry and very thirsty, but she would not tell Al her wants if she starved. She tried to guess at his plans and at his motive for taking her away like this. He had no camping outfit, a bulkily rolled slicker forming his only burden. He could not, then, be planning to take her much farther into the wilderness; yet if he did not hide her away, how could he expect to keep her? His motive for marrying her was rather mystifying. He did not seem sufficiently in love with her to warrant an abduction, and he was too cool for such a headlong action, unless driven by necessity. She wondered what he was thinking about as he rode. Not about her, she guessed, except when some bad place in the trail made it necessary for him to stop, tie Snake to the nearest bush, lead his own horse past the obstruction and come back after her. Several times this was necessary. Once he took the time to examine the thongs on her ankles, apparently wishing to make sure that she was not uncomfortable. Once he looked up into her sullenly distressed face and said, "Tired?" in a humanly sympathetic tone that made her blink back the tears. She shook her head and would not look at him. Al regarded her in silence for a minute, led Snake to his own horse, mounted and rode on.

He was a murderer; he had undoubtedly killed many men. He would kill her if she attempted to escape - "and he could not catch me," Lorraine was just enough to add. Yet she felt baffled; cheated of the full horror of being kidnapped.

She had no knowledge of a bad man who was human in spots without being repentant. For love of a girl, she had been taught to believe, the worst outlaw would weep over his past misdeeds, straighten his shoulders, look to heaven for help and become a self-sacrificing hero for whom audiences might be counted upon to shed furtive tears.

Al Woodruff, however, did not love her. His eyes had once or twice softened to friendliness, but love was not there. Neither was repentance there. He seemed quite satisfied with himself, quite ready to commit further crimes for sake of his own safety or desire. He was hard, she decided, but he was not unnecessarily harsh; cruel, without being wantonly brutal. He was, in short, the strangest man she had ever seen.

## CHAPTER TWENTY-ONE

## "OH, I COULD KILL YOU!"

Before sundown they reached the timberland on Bear Top. The horses slipped on the pine needles when Al left the trail and rode up a gentle incline where the trees grew large and there was little underbrush. It was very beautiful, with the slanting sun-rays painting broad yellow bars across the gloom of the forest. In a little while they reached the crest of that slope, and Lorraine, looking back, could only guess at where the trail wound on among the trees lower down.

Birds called companionably from the high branches above them. A nesting grouse flew chuttering out from under a juniper bush, alighted a short distance away and went limping and dragging one wing before them, cheeping piteously.

While Lorraine was wondering if the poor thing had hurt a leg in lighting, Al clipped its head off neatly with a bullet from his six-shooter, though Lorraine had not seen him pull the gun and did not know he meant to shoot. The bird's mate whirred up and away through the trees, and Lorraine was glad that it had escaped.

Al slid the gun back into his holster, leaned from his saddle and picked up the dead grouse as unconcernedly as he would have dismounted, pulled his knife from his boot and drew the bird neatly, flinging the crop and entrails from him.

"Them juniper berries tastes the meat if you don't clean 'em out right away," he remarked casually to Lorraine, as he wiped the knife on his trousers and thrust it back into the boot-scabbard before he tied the grouse to the saddle by its blue, scaley little feet.

When he was ready to go on, Snake refused to budge. Tough as he was, he had at last reached the limit of his energy and ambition. Al yanked hard on the bridle reins, then rode back and struck him sharply with his quirt before Snake would rouse himself enough to move forward. He went stiffly, reluctantly, pulling back until his head was held straight out before him. Al dragged him so for a rod or two, lost patience and returned to whip him forward again.

"What a brute you are!" Lorraine exclaimed indignantly. "Can't you see now tired he is?"

Al glanced at her from under his eyebrows. "He's all in, but he's got to make it," he said. "I've been that way myself - and made it. What I can do, a horse can do. Come on, you yella-livered bonehead!"

Snake went on, urged now and then by Al's quirt. Every blow made Lorraine wince, and she made the wincing perfectly apparent to Al, in the hope that he would take some notice of it and give her a chance to tell him what she thought of him without opening the conversation herself.

But Al did not say anything. When the time came - as even Lorraine saw that it must - when Snake refused to attempt a steep slope, Al still said nothing. He untied her ankles from the stirrups and her hands from the saddle horn, carried her in his arms to his own horse and compelled her to mount. Then he retied her exactly as she had been tied on Snake.

"Skinner knows this trail," he told Lorraine. "And I'm behind yuh with a gun. Don't forget that, Miss Spitfire. You let Skinner go to suit himself - and if he goes wrong, you pay, because it'll be you reining him wrong. Get along there, Skinner!"

Skinner got along in a businesslike way that told why Al Woodruff had chosen to ride him on this trip. He seemed to be a perfectly dependable saddle horse for a bandit to own. He wound in and out among the trees and boulders, stepping carefully over fallen logs; he thrust his nose out straight and laid back his ears and pushed his way through thickets of young pines; he went circumspectly along the edge of a deep gulch, climbed over a ridge and worked his way down the precipitous slope on the farther side, made his way around a thick clump of spruces and stopped in a little, grassy glade no bigger than a city lot, but with a spring gurgling somewhere near. Then he swung his head around and looked over his shoulder inquiringly at Al, who was coming behind, leading Snake.

Lorraine looked at him also, but Al did not say anything to her or to the horse. He let them stand there and wait while he unsaddled Snake, put a drag rope on him and led him to the best grazing. Then, coming back, he very matter-of-factly untied Lorraine and helped her off the horse. Lorraine was all prepared to fight, but she did not quite know how to struggle with a man who did not take hold of her or touch her, except to steady her in dismounting. Unconsciously she waited for a cue, and the cue was not given.

Al's mind seemed intent upon making Skinner comfortable. Still, he kept an eye on Lorraine, and he did not turn his back to her. Lorraine looked over to where Snake, too exhausted to eat, stood with drooping head and all four legs braced like sticks under him. It flashed across her mind that not even her old director would order her to make a run for that horse and try to get away on him. Snake looked as if he would never move from that position until he toppled over.

Al pulled the bridle off Skinner, gave him a half-affectionate slap on the rump, and watched him go off, switching his tail and nosing the ground for a likable place to roll. Al's glance went on to Snake, and from him to Lorraine.

"You sure do know how to ride hell out of a horse," he remarked.

"Now he'll be stiff and sore to-morrow - and we've got quite a ride to make."

His tone of disapproval sent a guilty feeling through Lorraine, until she remembered that a slow horse might save her from this man who was all bad, - except, perhaps, just on the surface which was not altogether repellent. She looked around at the tiny basin set like a saucer among the pines. Already the dusk was painting deep shadows in the woods across the opening, and turning the sky a darker blue. Skinner rolled over twice, got up and shook himself with a satisfied snort and went away to feed. She might, if she were patient, run to the horse when Al's back was turned, she thought. Once in the woods she might have some chance of eluding him, and perhaps Skinner would show as much wisdom going as he had in coming, and take her down to the sageland.

But Skinner walked to the farther edge of the meadow before he stopped, and Al Woodruff never turned his back to a foe. An owl hooted unexpectedly, and Lorraine edged closer to her captor, who was gathering dead branches one by one and throwing them toward a certain spot which he had evidently selected for a campfire. He looked at her keenly, even suspiciously, and pointed with the stick in his left hand.

"You might go over there by the saddle and set down till I get a fire going," he said. "Don't go wandering around aimless, like a hen turkey, watching a chance to duck into the brush. There's bear in there and lion and lynx, and I'd hate to see you chawed. They never clean their toe-nails, and blood poison generally sets in where they leave a scratch. Go and set down."

Lorraine did not know how much of his talk was truth, but she went and sat down by his saddle and began braiding her hair in two tight braids like a squaw. If she did get a chance to run, she thought, she did not want her hair flying loose to catch on bushes and briars. She had once fled through a brush patch in Griffith Park with her hair flowing loose, and she had not liked the experience, though it had looked very nice on the screen.

Before she had finished the braiding, Al came over to the saddle and untied his slicker roll and the grouse.

"Come on over to the fire," he said. "I'll learn yuh a trick or two about camp cooking. If I'm goin' to keep yuh with me, you might just as well learn how to cook. We'll be on the trail the biggest part of our time, I expect."

He took her by the arm, just as any man might have done, and led her to the fire that was beginning to crackle cheerfully. He set her down on the side where the smoke would be least likely to blow her way and proceeded to dress the grouse, stripping off skin and feathers together. He unrolled the slicker and laid out a piece of bacon, a package of coffee, a small coffeepot, bannock and salt. The coffeepot and the grouse he took in one hand - his left, Lorraine observed - and started toward the spring which she could hear gurgling in the shadows amongst the trees.

Lorraine watched him sidelong. He seemed to take it for granted now that she would stay where she was. The woods were dark, the firelight and the warmth enticed her. The sight of the supper preparations made her hungrier than she had ever been in her life before. When one has breakfasted on one cup of coffee at dawn and has ridden all day with nothing to eat, running away from food, even though that food is in the hands of one's captor, requires courage. Lorraine was terribly tempted to stay, at least until she had eaten. But Al might not give her another chance like this. She crept on her knees to the slicker and seized one piece of bannock, crawled out of the firelight stealthily, then sprang to her feet and began running straight across the meadow toward Skinner.

Twenty yards she covered when a bullet sang over her head. Lorraine ducked, stumbled and fell headfirst over a hummock, not quite sure that she had not been shot.

"Thought maybe I could trust yuh to play square," Al said disgustedly, pulling her to her feet, the gun still smoking in his hands. "You little fool, what do you think you'd do in these hills alone? You sure enough belittle me, if you think you'd have a chance in a million of getting away from me!"

She fought him, then, with a great, inner relief that the situation was at last swinging around to a normal kidnapping. Still, Al Woodruff seemed unable to play his part realistically. He failed to fill her with fear and repulsion. She had to think back, to remember that he had killed men, in order to realize her own danger. Now, for instance, he merely forced her back to the campfire, pulled the saddle strings from his pocket and tied her feet together, using a complicated knot which he told her she might work on all she darn pleased, for all he cared. Then he went calmly to work cooking their supper.

This was simple. He divided the grouse so that one part had the meaty breast and legs, and the other the back and wings. The meaty part he larded neatly with strips of bacon, using his hunting knife, - which Lorraine watched fascinatedly, wondering if it had ever taken the life of a man. He skewered the meat on a green, forked stick and gave it to her to broil for herself over the hottest coals of the fire, while he made the coffee and prepared his own portion of the grouse.

Lorraine was hungry. She broiled the grouse carefully and ate it, with the exception of one leg, which she surprised herself by offering to Al, who was picking the bones of his own share down to the last shred of meat. She drank a cup of coffee, black, and returned the cup to the killer, who unconcernedly drank from it without any previous rinsing. She ate bannock with her meat and secretly thought what an adventure it would be if only it were not real, - if only she were not threatened with a forced marriage to this man. The primitive camp appealed to her; she who had prided herself upon being an outdoor girl saw how she had always played at being primitive. This was real. She would have loved it if only the man opposite were Lone, or Swan, or some one else whom she knew and trusted.

She watched the firelight dancing on Al's somber face, softening its hardness, making it almost wistful when he gazed thoughtfully into the coals. She thrilled when she saw how watchful he was, how he lifted his head and listened to every little night sound. She was afraid of him as she feared the lightning; she feared his pitiless attitude toward human life. She would find some way to outwit him when it came to the point of marrying him, she thought. She would escape him if she could without too great a risk of being shot. She felt absolutely certain that he would shoot her with as little compunction as he would marry her by force, - and it seemed to Lorraine that he would not greatly care which he did.

"I guess you're tired," Al said suddenly, rousing himself from deep study and looking at her imperturbably. "I'll fix yuh so you can sleep - and that's about all yuh can do."

He went over to his saddle, took the blanket and unfolded it until Lorraine saw that it was a full-size bed blanket of heavy gray wool. The man's ingenuity seemed endless. Without seeming to have any extra luggage, he had nevertheless carried a very efficient camp outfit with him. He took his hunting knife, went to the spruce grove and cut many small, green branches, returning with all he could hold in his arms. She watched him lay them tips up for a mattress, and was secretly glad that she knew this much at least of camp comfort. He spread the blanket over them and then, without a word, came over to her and untied her feet.

"Go and lay down on the blanket," he commanded.

"I'll do nothing of the kind!" Lorraine set her mouth stubbornly.

"Well, then I'll have to lay you down," said Al, lifting her to her feet. "If you get balky, I'm liable to get rough."

Lorraine drew away from him as far as she could and looked at him for a full minute. Al stared back into her eyes. "Oh, I could *kill* you!" cried Lorraine for the second time that day and threw herself down on the bed, sobbing like an angry child.

Al said nothing. The man's capacity for keeping still was amazing. He knelt beside her, folded the blanket over her from the two sides, and tied the corners around her neck snugly, the knot at the back. In the same way he tied her ankles. Lorraine found herself in a sleeping bag from which she had small hope of extricating herself. He took his coat, folded it compactly and pushed it under her head for a pillow; then he brought her own saddle blanket and spread it over her for extra warmth.

"Now stop your bawling and go to sleep," he advised her calmly. "You ain't hurt, and you ain't going to be as long as you gentle down and behave yourself."

She saw him draw the slicker over his shoulders and move back where the shadows were deep and she could not see him. She heard some animal squall in the woods behind them. She looked up at the stars, - millions of them, and brighter than she had ever seen them before. Insensibly she quieted, watching the stars, listening to the night noises, catching now and then a whiff of smoke from Al Woodruff's cigarette. Before she knew that she was sleepy, she slept.

## CHAPTER TWENTY-TWO

## "YACK, I LICK YOU GOOD IF YOU BARK"

Swan cooked himself a hasty meal while he studied the various possibilities of the case and waited for further word from headquarters. He wanted to be sure that help had started and to be able to estimate within an hour or two the probable time of its arrival, before he left the wireless. Jack he fed and left on watch outside the cabin, so that he could without risk keep open the door to the dugout.

His instrument was not a large one, and the dugout door was thick, - as a precaution against discovery if he should be called when some visitor chanced to be in the cabin. Not often did a man ride that way, though occasionally some one stopped for a meal if he knew that the cabin was there and had ever tasted Swan's sour-dough biscuits. His aerial was cleverly camouflaged between the two pine trees, and he had no fear of discovery there; Jack was a faithful guardian and would give warning if any one approached the place. Swan could therefore give his whole attention to the business at hand.

He was not yet supplied with evidence enough to warrant arresting Warfield and Hawkins, but he hoped to get it when the real crisis came. They could not have known of Al Woodruff's intentions toward Lorraine, else they would have kept themselves in the background and would not have risked the failure of their own plan.

On the other hand, Al must have been wholly ignorant of Warfield's scheme to try and prove Lorraine crazy. It looked to Swan very much like a muddling of the Sawtooth affairs through over-anxiety to avoid trouble. They were afraid of what Lorraine knew. They wanted to eliminate her, and they had made the blunder of working independently to that end.

Lone's anxiety he did not even consider. He believed that Lone would be equal to any immediate emergency and would do whatever the circumstances seemed to require of him. Warfield counted him a Sawtooth man. Al Woodruff, if the four men met unexpectedly, would also take it for granted that he was one of them. They would probably talk to Lone without reserve, - Swan counted on that. Whereas, if he were present, they would be on their guard, at least.

Swan's plan was to wait at the cabin until he knew that deputies were headed toward the Pass. Then, with Jack, it would be a simple matter to follow Warfield to where he overtook Al, - supposing he did overtake him. If he did not, then Swan meant to be present when the meeting occurred. The dog would trail Al anywhere, since the scent would be less than twenty-four hours old. Swan would locate Warfield and lead him straight to Al Woodruff, and then make his arrests. But he wanted to have the deputies there.

At dusk he got his call. He learned that four picked men had started for the Pass, and that they would reach the divide by daybreak. Others were on their way to intercept Al Woodruff if he crossed before then.

It was all that Swan could have hoped for, - more than he had dared to expect on such short notice. He notified the operator that he would not be there to receive anything else, until he returned to report that he had got his men.

"Don't count your chickens till they're hatched," came facetiously out of the blue.

"By golly, I can hear them holler in the shell," Swan sent back, grinning to himself as he rattled the key. "That irrigation graft is killed now. You tell the boss Swan says so. He's right. The way to catch a fox is to watch his den."

He switched off the current, closed the case and went out, making sure that the cupboard-camouflaged door looked perfectly innocent on the outside. With a bannock stuffed into one pocket, a chunk of bacon in the other, he left the cabin and swung off again in that long, tireless stride of his, Jack following contentedly at his heels.

At the farther end of Skyline Meadow he stopped, took a tough leather leash from his pocket and fastened it to Jack's collar.

"We don't go running to paw nobody's stomach and say, 'Wow-wow! Here we are back again!'" he told the dog, pulling its ears affectionately. "Maybe we get shot or something like that. We trail, and we keep our mouth still, Yack. One bark, and I lick you good!"

Jack flashed out a pink tongue and licked his master's chin to show how little he was worried over the threat, and went racing along at the end of the leash, taking Swan's trail and his own back to where they had climbed out of the canyon.

At the bottom Swan spoke to the dog in an undertone, and Jack obediently started up the canyon on the trail of the five horses who had passed that way since noon. It was starlight now, and Swan did not hurry. He was taking it for granted that Warfield and Hawkins would stop when it became too dark to follow the hoofprints, and without Jack to show them the way they would perforce remain where they were until daybreak.

They would do that, he reasoned, if they were sincere in wanting to overtake Lorraine and in their ignorance that they were also following Al Woodruff. And try as he would, he could not see the object of so foolish a plan as this abduction carried out in collusion with two men of unknown sentiments in the party.

They had shown no suspicion of Al's part in the affair, and Swan grinned when he thought of the mutual surprise when they met.

He was not disappointed. They reached timber line, following the seldom used trail that wound over the divide to Bear Top Pass and so, by a difficult route which he did not believe Al would attempt after dark, to the country beyond the mountain. Where dark overtook them, they stopped in a sheltered nook to wait, just as Swan had expected they would. They were close to the trail, where no one could pass without their knowledge.

In the belief that it was only Lorraine they were following, and that she would be frightened and would come to the cheer of a campfire, they had a fine, inviting blaze. Swan made his way as close as he dared, without being discovered, and sat down to wait. He could see nothing of the men until Lone appeared and fed the flames more wood, and sat down where the light shone on his face. Swan grinned again. Warfield had probably decided that Lorraine would be less afraid of Lone than of them and had ordered him into the firelight as a sort of decoy. And Lone, knowing that Al Woodruff might be within shooting distance, was probably much more uncomfortable than he looked.

He sat with his legs crossed in true range fashion and stared into the fire while he smoked. He was a fair mark for an enemy who might be lurking out there in the dark, but he gave no sign that he realized the danger of his position. Neither did he wear any air of expectancy. Warfield and Hawkins might wait and listen and hope that Lorraine, wide-eyed and weary, would steal up to the warmth of the fire; but not Lone.

Swan, sitting on a rotting log, became uneasy at the fine target which Lone made by the fire, and drew Al Woodruff's blue bandanna from his pocket. He held it to Jack's nose and whispered, "You find him, Yack - and I lick you good if you bark." Jack sniffed, dropped his nose to the ground and began tugging at the leash. Swan got up and, moving stealthily, followed the dog.

## CHAPTER TWENTY-THREE

## "I COULDA LOVED THIS LITTLE GIRL"

A chill wind that hurried over Bear Top ahead of the dawn brought Swan and Jack clattering up the trail that dipped into Spirit Canyon. Warfield rose stiffly from the one-sided warmth of the fire and walked a few paces to meet him, shrugging his wide shoulders at the cold and rubbing his thigh muscles that protested against movement. Much riding upon upholstered cushions had not helped Senator Warfield to retain the tough muscles of hard-riding Bill Warfield. The senator was saddle-sore as well as hungry, and his temper showed in his blood-shot eyes. He would have quarreled with his best-beloved woman that morning, and he began on Swan.

Why hadn't he come back down the gulch yesterday and helped track the girl, as he was told to do? (The senator had quite unpleasant opinions of Swedes, and crazy women, and dogs that were never around when they were wanted, and he expressed them fluently.)

Swan explained with a great deal of labor that he had not thought he was wanted, and that he had to sleep on his claim sometimes or the law would take it from him, maybe. Also he virtuously pointed out that he had come with Yack before daylight to the canyon to see if they had found Miss Hunter and gone home, or if they were still hunting for her.

"If you like to find that jong lady, I put Yack on the trail quick," he offered placatingly. "I bet you Yack finds her in one-half an hour."

With much unnecessary language, Senator Warfield told him to get to work, and the three tightened cinches, mounted their horses and prepared to follow Swan's lead. Swan watched his chance and gave Lone a chunk of bannock as a substitute for breakfast, and Lone, I may add, dropped behind his companions and ate every crumb of it, in spite of his worry over Lorraine.

Indeed, Swan eased that worry too, when they were climbing the pine slope where Al had killed the grouse. Lone had forged ahead on John Doe, and Swan stopped suddenly, pointing to the spot where a few bloody feathers and a boot-print showed. The other evidence Jack had eaten in the night.

"Raine's all right, Lone. Got men coming. Keep your gun handy," he murmured and turned away as the others rode up, eager for whatever news Swan had to offer.

"Something killed a bird," Swan explained politely, planting one of his own big feet over the track, which did not in the least resemble Lorraine's. "Yack! you find that jong lady quick!"

From there on Swan walked carefully, putting his foot wherever a print of Al's boot was visible. Since he was much bigger than Al, with a correspondingly longer stride, his gait puzzled Lone until he saw just what Swan was doing. Then his eyes lightened with amused appreciation of the Swede's cunning.

"We ought to have some hot drink, or whisky, when we find that girl," Hawkins muttered unexpectedly, riding up beside Lone as they crossed an open space. "She'll be half-dead with cold - if we find her alive."

Before Lone could answer, Swan looked back at the two and raised his hand for them to stop.

"Better if you leave the horses here," he suggested. "From Yack I know we get close pretty quick. That jong lady's horse maybe smells these horse and makes a noise, and crazy folks run from noise."

Without objection the three dismounted and tied their horses securely to trees. Then, with Swan and Jack leading the way, they climbed over the ridge and descended into the hollow by way of the ledge which Skinner had negotiated so carefully the night before. Without the dog they never would have guessed that any one had passed this way, but as it was they made good progress and reached the nearest edge of the spruce thicket just as the sun was making ready to push up over the skyline.

Jack stopped and looked up at his master inquiringly, lifting his lip at the sides and showing his teeth. But he made no sound; nor did Swan, when he dropped his fingers to the dog's head and patted him approvingly.

They heard a horse sneeze, beyond the spruce grove, and Warfield stepped forward authoritatively, waving Swan back. This, his manner said plainly, was first and foremost his affair, and from now on he would take charge of the situation. At his heels went Hawkins, and Swan sent an oblique glance of satisfaction toward Lone, who answered it with his half-smile. Swan himself could not have planned the approach more to his liking.

The smell of bacon cooking watered their mouths and made Warfield and Hawkins look at one another inquiringly. Crazy young women would hardly be expected to carry a camping outfit. But Swan and Lone were treading close on their heels, and their own curiosity pulled them forward. They went carefully around the thicket, guided by the pungent odor of burning pine wood, and halted so abruptly that Swan and Lone bumped into them from behind. A man had risen up from the campfire and faced them, his hands rising slowly, palms outward.

"Warfield, by - !" Al blurted in his outraged astonishment. "Trailing me with a bunch, are yuh? I knew you'd double-cross your own father - but I never thought you had it in you to do it in the open. Damn yuh, what d'yuh want that you expect to get?"

Warfield stared at him, slack-jawed. He glanced furtively behind him at Swan, and found that guileless youth ready to poke him in the back with the muzzle of a gun. Lone, he observed, had another. He looked back at Al, whose eyes were ablaze with resentment. With an effort he smiled his disarming, senatorial smile, but Al's next words froze it on his face.

"I think I know the play you're making, but it won't get you anything, Bill Warfield. You think I slipped up - and you told me not to let my foot slip; said you'd hate to lose me. Well, you're the one that slipped, you damned, rotten coward. I was watching out for leaks. I stopped two, and this one -"

He glanced down at Lorraine, who sat beside the fire, a blanket tied tightly around her waist and her ankles, so that, while comfortably free, she could make no move to escape.

"I was fixing to stop *her* from telling all she knew," he added harshly. "By to-night I'd have had her married to me, you damned fool. And here you've blocked everything for me, afraid I was falling down on my job!

"Now folks, lemme just tell you a few little things. I know my limit - you've got me dead to rights. I ain't complaining about that; a man in my game expects to get his, some day. But I ain't going to let the man go that paid me my wages and a bonus of five hundred dollars for every man I killed that he wanted outa the way.

"Hawkins knows that's a fact. He's foreman of the Sawtooth, and he knows the agreement. I've got to say for Hawkins that aside from stealing cattle off the nesters and helping make evidence against some that's in jail, Hawkins never done any dirty work. He didn't have to. They paid *me* for that end of the business.

"I killed Fred Thurman - this girl, here, saw me shoot him. And it was when I told Warfield I was afraid she might set folks talking that he began to get cold feet. Up to then everything was lovely, but Warfield began to crawfish a little. We figured - *we* figured, emphasize the *we*, folks, - that the Quirt would have to be put outa business. We knew if the girl told Brit and Frank, they'd maybe get the nerve to try and pin something on us. We've stole 'em blind for years, and they wouldn't cry if we got hung. Besides, they was friendly with Fred.

"The girl and the Swede got in the way when I tried to bump Brit off. I'd have gone into the canyon and finished him with a rock, but they beat me to it. The girl herself I couldn't get at very well and make it look accidental - and anyway, I never did kill a woman, and I'd hate it like hell. I figured if her dad got killed, she'd leave.

"And let me tell you, folks, Warfield raised hell with me because Brit Hunter wasn't killed when he pitched over the grade. He held out on me for that job - so I'm collecting five hundred dollars' worth of fun right now. He did say he'd pay me after Brit was dead, but it looks like he's going to pull through, so I ain't counting much on getting my money outa Warfield.

"Frank I got, and made a clean job of it. And yesterday morning the girl played into my hands. She rode over to the Sawtooth, and I got her at Thurman's place, on her way home, and figured I'd marry her and take a chance on keeping her quiet afterwards. I'd have been down the Pass in another two hours and heading for the nearest county seat. She'd have married me, too. She knows I'd have killed her if she didn't - which I would. I've been square with her - she'll tell you that. I told her, when I took her, just what I was going to do with her. So that's all straight. She's been scared, I guess, but she ain't gone hungry, and she ain't suffered, except in her mind. I don't fight women, and I'll say right now, to her and to you, that I've got all the respect in the world for this little girl, and if I'd married her I'd have been as good to her as I know how, and as she'd let me be.

"Now I want to tell you folks a few more things about Bill Warfield. If you want to stop the damnest steal in the country, tie a can onto that irrigation scheme of his. He's out to hold up the State for all he can get, and bleed the poor devils of farmers white, that buys land under that canal. It may look good, but it ain't good - not by a damn sight.

"Yuh know what he's figuring on doing? Get water in the canal, sell land under a contract that lets him out if the ditch breaks, or something so he *can't* supply water at any time. And when them poor suckers gets their crops all in, and at the point where they've got to have water or lose out, something'll happen to the supply. Folks, I *know*! I'm a reliable man, and I've rode with a rope around my neck for over five years, and Warfield offered me the same old five hundred every time I monkeyed with the water supply as ordered. He'd have done it slick; don't worry none about that. The biggest band of thieves he could get together is that company. So if you folks have got any sense, you'll bust it up right now.

"Bill Warfield, what I've got to say to *you* won't take long. You thought you'd make a grand-stand play with the law, and at the same time put me outa the way. You figured I'd resist arrest, and you'd have a chance to shoot me down. I know your rotten mind better than you do. You wanted to bump me off, but you wanted to do it in a way that'd put you in right with the public. Killing me for kidnapping this girl would sound damn romantic in the newspapers, and it wouldn't have a thing to do with Thurman or Frank Johnson, or any of the rest that I've sent over the trail for you.

"Right now you're figuring how you'll get around this bawling-out I'm giving you. There's nobody to take down what I say, and I'm just a mean, ornery outlaw and killer, talking for spite. With your pull you expect to get this smoothed over and hushed up, and have me at a hanging bee, and everything all right for Bill! Well -"

His eyes left Warfield's face and went beyond the staring group. His face darkened, a sneer twisted his lips.

"Who're them others?" he cried harshly. "Was you afraid four wouldn't be enough to take me?"

The four turned heads to look. Bill Warfield never looked back, for Al's gun spoke, and Warfield sagged at the knees and the shoulders, and he slumped to the ground at the instant when Al's gun spoke again.

"That's for you, Lone Morgan," Al cried, as he fired again. "She talked about you in her sleep last night. She called you Loney, and she wanted you to come and get her. I was going to kill you first chance I got. I coulda loved this little girl. I - could -"

He was down, bleeding and coughing and trying to talk. Swan had shot him, and two of the deputies who had been there through half of Al's bitter talk. Lorraine, unable to get up and run, too sturdy of soul to faint, had rolled over and away from him, her lips held tightly together, her eyes wide with horror. Al crawled after her, his eyes pleading.

"Little Spitfire - I shot your Loney - but I'd have been good to you, girl. I watched yuh all night - and I couldn't help loving yuh. I - couldn't -" That was all. Within three feet of her, his face toward her and his eyes agonizing to meet hers, he died.

## CHAPTER TWENTY-FOUR

## ANOTHER STORY BEGINS

This chapter is very much like a preface: it is not absolutely necessary, although many persons will read it and a few will be glad that it was written.

The story itself is ended. To go on would be to begin another story; to tell of the building up of the Quirt outfit, with Lone and Lone's savings playing a very important part, and with Brit a semi-invalided, retired stockman who smoked his pipe and told the young couple what they should do and how they should do it.

Frank he mourned for and seldom mentioned. The Sawtooth, under the management of a greatly chastened young Bob Warfield, was slowly winning its way back to the respect of its neighbors.

For certain personal reasons there was no real neighborliness between the Quirt and the Sawtooth. There could not be, so long as Brit's memory remained clear, and Bob was every day reminded of the crimes his father had paid a man to commit. Moreover, Southerners are jealous of their women, - it is their especial prerogative. And Lone suspected that, given the opportunity, Bob Warfield would have fallen in love with Lorraine. Indeed, he suspected that any man in the country would have done that. Al Woodruff had, and he was noted for his indifference to women and his implacable hardness toward men.

But you are not to accuse Lone of being a jealous husband. He was not, and I am merely pointing out the fact that he might have been, had he been given any cause.

Oh, by the way, Swan "proved up" as soon as possible on his homestead and sold out to the Quirt. Lone managed to buy the Thurman ranch also, and the TJ up-and-down is on its feet again as a cattle ranch. Sorry and Jim will ride for the Quirt, I suppose, as long as they can crawl into a saddle, but there are younger men now to ride the Skyline Meadow range.

Some one asked about Yellowjacket, having, I suppose, a sneaking regard for his infirmities. He hasn't been peeled yet - or he hadn't, the last I heard of him. Lone and Lorraine told me they were trying to save him for the "Little Feller" to practise on when he is able to sit up without a cushion behind his back, and to hold something besides a rubber rattle. And - oh, do you know how Lone is teaching the Little Feller to sit up on the floor? He took a horse collar and scrubbed it until he nearly wore out the leather. Then he brought it to the cabin, put it on the floor and set the Little Feller inside it.

They sent me a snap-shot of the event, but it is not very good. The film was under-exposed, and nothing was to be seen of the Little Feller except a hazy spot which I judged was a hand, holding a black object I guessed was the ridgy, rubber rattle with the whistle gone out of the end, - down the Little Feller's throat, they are afraid. And there was his smile, and a glimpse of his eyes.

Aren't you envious as sin, and glad they're so happy?

# Choose from Thousands of 1stWorldLibrary Classics By

A. M. Barnard
Ada Leverson
Adolphus William Ward
Aesop
Agatha Christie
Alexander Aaronsohn
Alexander Kielland
Alexandre Dumas
Alfred Gatty
Alfred Ollivant
Alice Duer Miller
Alice Turner Curtis
Alice Dunbar
Allen Chapman
Ambrose Bierce
Amelia E. Barr
Amory H. Bradford
Andrew Lang
Andrew McFarland Davis
Andy Adams
Anna Alice Chapin
Anna Sewell
Annie Besant
Annie Hamilton Donnell
Annie Payson Call
Annie Roe Carr
Annonaymous
Anton Chekhov
Arnold Bennett
Arthur Conan Doyle
Arthur M. Winfield
Arthur Ransome
Arthur Schnitzler
Atticus
B.H. Baden-Powell
B. M. Bower
B. C. Chatterjee
Baroness Emmuska Orczy
Baroness Orczy
Basil King
Bayard Taylor
Ben Macomber
Bertha Muzzy Bower
Bjornstjerne Bjornson
Booth Tarkington
Boyd Cable
Bram Stoker
C. Collodi
C. E. Orr
C. M. Ingleby
Carolyn Wells
Catherine Parr Traill
Charles A. Eastman
Charles Amory Beach
Charles Dickens
Charles Dudley Warner
Charles Farrar Browne
Charles Ives
Charles Kingsley
Charles Klein
Charles Hanson Towne
Charles Lathrop Pack
Charles Romyn Dake
Charles Whibley
Charles Willing Beale
Charlotte M. Braeme
Charlotte M. Yonge
Charlotte Perkins Stetson
Clair W. Hayes
Clarence Day Jr.
Clarence E. Mulford
Clemence Housman
Confucius
Coningsby Dawson
Cornelis DeWitt Wilcox
Cyril Burleigh
D. H. Lawrence
Daniel Defoe
David Garnett
Dinah Craik
Don Carlos Janes
Donald Keyhoe
Dorothy Kilner
Dougan Clark
Douglas Fairbanks
E. Nesbit
E.P.Roe
E. Phillips Oppenheim
Earl Barnes
Edgar Rice Burroughs
Edith Van Dyne
Edith Wharton
Edward Everett Hale
Edward J. O'Biren
Edward S. Ellis
Edwin L. Arnold
Eleanor Atkins
Eliot Gregory
Elizabeth Gaskell
Elizabeth McCracken
Elizabeth Von Arnim
Ellem Key
Emerson Hough
Emilie F. Carlen
Emily Dickinson
Enid Bagnold
Enilor Macartney Lane
Erasmus W. Jones
Ernie Howard Pie
Ethel May Dell
Ethel Turner
Ethel Watts Mumford
Eugenie Foa
Eugene Wood
Eustace Hale Ball
Evelyn Everett-green
Everard Cotes
F. H. Cheley
F. J. Cross
F. Marion Crawford
Federick Austin Ogg
Ferdinand Ossendowski
Francis Bacon
Francis Darwin
Frances Hodgson Burnett
Frances Parkinson Keyes
Frank Gee Patchin
Frank Harris
Frank Jewett Mather
Frank L. Packard
Frank V. Webster
Frederic Stewart Isham
Frederick Trevor Hill
Frederick Winslow Taylor
Friedrich Kerst
Friedrich Nietzsche
Fyodor Dostoyevsky
G.A. Henty
G.K. Chesterton
Gabrielle E. Jackson
Garrett P. Serviss
Gaston Leroux
George A. Warren
George Ade
Geroge Bernard Shaw
George Durston
George Ebers

| | | |
|---|---|---|
| George Eliot | Herbert Carter | John Habberton |
| George Gissing | Herbert N. Casson | John Joy Bell |
| George MacDonald | Herman Hesse | John Kendrick Bangs |
| George Meredith | Hildegard G. Frey | John Milton |
| George Orwell | Homer | John Philip Sousa |
| George Sylvester Viereck | Honore De Balzac | Jonas Lauritz Idemil Lie |
| George Tucker | Horace B. Day | Jonathan Swift |
| George W. Cable | Horace Walpole | Joseph A. Altsheler |
| George Wharton James | Horatio Alger Jr. | Joseph Carey |
| Gertrude Atherton | Howard Pyle | Joseph Conrad |
| Gordon Casserly | Howard R. Garis | Joseph E. Badger Jr |
| Grace E. King | Hugh Lofting | Joseph Hergesheimer |
| Grace Gallatin | Hugh Walpole | Joseph Jacobs |
| Grace Greenwood | Humphry Ward | Jules Vernes |
| Grant Allen | Ian Maclaren | Julian Hawthrone |
| Guillermo A. Sherwell | Inez Haynes Gillmore | Julie A Lippmann |
| Gulielma Zollinger | Irving Bacheller | Justin Huntly McCarthy |
| Gustav Flaubert | Isabel Hornibrook | Kakuzo Okakura |
| H. A. Cody | Israel Abrahams | Kenneth Grahame |
| H. B. Irving | Ivan Turgenev | Kenneth McGaffey |
| H.C. Bailey | J.G.Austin | Kate Langley Bosher |
| H. G. Wells | J. Henri Fabre | Kate Langley Bosher |
| H. H. Munro | J. M. Barrie | Katherine Cecil Thurston |
| H. Irving Hancock | J. Macdonald Oxley | Katherine Stokes |
| H. Rider Haggard | J. S. Fletcher | L. A. Abbot |
| H. W. C. Davis | J. S. Knowles | L. T. Meade |
| Haldeman Julius | J. Storer Clouston | L. Frank Baum |
| Hall Caine | Jack London | Latta Griswold |
| Hamilton Wright Mabie | Jacob Abbott | Laura Dent Crane |
| Hans Christian Andersen | James Allen | Laura Lee Hope |
| Harold Avery | James Andrews | Laurence Housman |
| Harold McGrath | James Baldwin | Lawrence Beasley |
| Harriet Beecher Stowe | James Branch Cabell | Leo Tolstoy |
| Harry Castlemon | James DeMille | Leonid Andreyev |
| Harry Coghill | James Joyce | Lewis Carroll |
| Harry Houdini | James Lane Allen | Lewis Sperry Chafer |
| Hayden Carruth | James Lane Allen | Lilian Bell |
| Helent Hunt Jackson | James Oliver Curwood | Lloyd Osbourne |
| Helen Nicolay | James Oppenheim | Louis Hughes |
| Hendrik Conscience | James Otis | Louis Tracy |
| Hendy David Thoreau | James R. Driscoll | Louisa May Alcott |
| Henri Barbusse | Jane Austen | Lucy Fitch Perkins |
| Henrik Ibsen | Jane L. Stewart | Lucy Maud Montgomery |
| Henry Adams | Janet Aldridge | Luther Benson |
| Henry Ford | Jens Peter Jacobsen | Lydia Miller Middleton |
| Henry Frost | Jerome K Jerome | Lyndon Orr |
| Henry James | John Burroughs | M. Corvus |
| Henry Jones Ford | John Cournos | M. H. Adams |
| Henry Seton Merriman | John F. Kennedy | Margaret E. Sangster |
| Henry W Longfellow | John Gay | Margret Howth |
| Herbert A. Giles | John Glasworthy | Margaret Vandercook |

Margret Penrose
Maria Edgeworth
Maria Thompson Daviess
Mariano Azuela
Marion Polk Angellotti
Mark Overton
Mark Twain
Mary Austin
Mary Catherine Crowley
Mary Cole
Mary Hastings Bradley
Mary Roberts Rinehart
Mary Rowlandson
M. Wollstonecraft Shelley
Maud Lindsay
Max Beerbohm
Myra Kelly
Nathaniel Hawthrone
Nicolo Machiavelli
O. F. Walton
Oscar Wilde
Owen Johnson
P.G. Wodehouse
Paul and Mabel Thorne
Paul G. Tomlinson
Paul Severing
Percy Brebner
Peter B. Kyne
Plato
R. Derby Holmes
R. L. Stevenson
R. S. Ball
Rabindranath Tagore
Rahul Alvares
Ralph Bonehill
Ralph Henry Barbour
Ralph Victor
Ralph Waldo Emmerson
Rene Descartes
Rex Beach

Rex E. Beach
Richard Harding Davis
Richard Jefferies
Richard Le Gallienne
Robert Barr
Robert Frost
Robert Gordon Anderson
Robert L. Drake
Robert Lansing
Robert Lynd
Robert Michael Ballantyne
Robert W. Chambers
Rosa Nouchette Carey
Rudyard Kipling
Samuel B. Allison
Samuel Hopkins Adams
Sarah Bernhardt
Sarah C. Hallowell
Selma Lagerlof
Sherwood Anderson
Sigmund Freud
Standish O'Grady
Stanley Weyman
Stella Benson
Stella M. Francis
Stephen Crane
Stewart Edward White
Stijn Streuvels
Swami Abhedananda
Swami Parmananda
T. S. Ackland
T. S. Arthur
The Princess Der Ling
Thomas A. Janvier
Thomas A Kempis
Thomas Anderton
Thomas Bailey Aldrich
Thomas Bulfinch
Thomas De Quincey
Thomas Dixon

Thomas H. Huxley
Thomas Hardy
Thomas More
Thornton W. Burgess
U. S. Grant
Valentine Williams
Various Authors
Vaughan Kester
Victor Appleton
Victoria Cross
Virginia Woolf
Wadsworth Camp
Walter Camp
Walter Scott
Washington Irving
Wilbur Lawton
Wilkie Collins
Willa Cather
Willard F. Baker
William Dean Howells
William le Queux
W. Makepeace Thackeray
William W. Walter
William Shakespeare
Winston Churchill
Yei Theodora Ozaki
Yogi Ramacharaka
Young E. Allison
Zane Grey

www.ingramcontent.com/pod-product-compliance
Lightning Source LLC
Chambersburg PA
CBHW022358040426
42450CB00005B/232